PRAISE FOR *JESUS MANIFESTO*

This is a really exhilarating reintroduction to a Jesus who seems sometimes to have become a stranger to the church; a passionate and joyful celebration of God with us, which cuts right through churchy quarrelling and brings us back to wonder, love, and praise—and the urgent desire to make Him known to all.

> — **Rowan Williams**
> Archbishop of Canterbury

Of all the doctrines, debates, and decisions throughout the history of Christianity, none has ever been as important as what we do with one simple question posed by Christ: "Who do *you* say that I am?" It is with this question that Leonard Sweet and Frank Viola begin a journey with the reader that leads to the very essence of the Christian faith.

Whether you are a seminary professor or someone seeking answers about Christ for the first time, *Jesus Manifesto* promises to illuminate the truth about the greatest personality to ever walk the earth. And along the way you will rediscover, or experience for the first time, the power, prestige and primacy of Jesus Christ.

> — **Ed Young**
> Pastor, Fellowship Church
> Author, *Outrageous, Contagious Joy*

There cannot be enough books written about the majesties and excellencies of Christ. To see Jesus as He is will transform us from one degree or glory to the next. Everything is about Him, for Him, and to Him. I am grateful that Frank and Leonard did the work and are putting this in the lap of so many.

> — **Matt Chandler**
> Lead Pastor, The Village Church

Today's church desperately needs that trumpet-like "certain sound" heard when Jesus' own voice is heard—just as He spoke in the Revelation. Our hour is similar to that; one of doctrinal drift, double entendre, and deepening deception, both in the church as in the world. *Jesus Manifesto* calls us to Jesus' person and position as Lord of the church, to hear Him call us to truth's clarity, power's purity, and obedience's reward, to restore that "saltness" that will keep *His* church alive and penetrating in its impact.

> — **Jack W. Hayford**
> Founding Pastor, The Church
> On the Way
> Chancellor, The King's Seminary

I look for books that call us to love Jesus and make His name more widely known. In *Jesus Manifesto*, Sweet and Viola ask us to step away out of the "Youniverse" (their word) of narcissistic religion and away from the pop-culture Jesus who is just a nice man. Throughout the book, they exalt Jesus as the divine Savior and ask the church to do the same. I believe this book will spark a renewed love for Christ by pointing us to the deep mystery of His person. You will be motivated to love and serve more deeply as your life is focused on Jesus the Messiah.

— **Ed Stetzer**
President, LifeWay Research

Brilliant, refreshing, soaring—and that's just the first chapter! This book is destined to be a classic devotional volume that will inspire generations of Jesus-followers. The line from the song goes, "you can have all this world, but give me Jesus." This book does just that.

— **Reggie McNeal**
Missional Leadership Specialist,
Leadership Network
Author, *The Present Future* and
Missional Renaissance

Jesus Manifesto is the most powerful work on Christ I have read in recent years. The Christ of the Empty Tomb is back among us. Sweet and Viola have beckoned us to return back to Olivet and renew our souls. I was hushed by its welcome authority. I found a lump in my throat as I read through page after page of Biblical witness to the one and only, incomparable Christ in whom alone is our Salvation. You must read this book. All of us must, and then we must believe in this book, rise, and advance on our culture with the truth we have lately backed away from in our faulty attempt to play fair at the cost of our God-given mission.

— **Calvin Miller**
Professor of Preaching and Pastoral
Ministry, Beeson Divinity
School, Birmingham, AL
Author, *Preaching: The Art of
Narrative Exposition*

One more sign of a Christianity that is beginning to look like Jesus again. Our great challenge over the past few decades has not been one of right believing but of right living. Viola and Sweet create a harmony here that invites you to give the world a Christianity worth believing in. After all, they will know we are Christians, not by our bumper stickers and t-shirts, but by our love.

— **Shane Claiborne**
Author, Activist, and Recovering
Sinner

From beginning to end, authentic Christianity is all about Jesus and, ultimately, nothing but Jesus. No one has proclaimed this more clearly and persuasively than Viola and Sweet. *Jesus Manifesto* is an important and powerful prophetic call for the Martha-like Church to get back to doing "the one thing that is needful."

— **Dr. Gregory A. Boyd**
Senior Pastor, Woodland Hills
Church, Maplewood, MN
Author, *Present Perfect, The Myth
of a Christian Nation*, and *The
Jesus Legend*.

Jesus Manifesto is a passionate invitation to fall head over heels in love with the Son of God. Prepare to be shaken. Prepare to be awakened. And prepare to answer the call to follow Jesus with wholehearted abandon. After reading this book, you'll never be the same.

— **Margaret Feinberg**
Author, *Scouting the Divine*

I love this book simply because I love Jesus. It will deepen, widen, and heighten your love for Christ; and few books can make that claim.

— **Mark Batterson**
Lead Pastor, National
Community Church
Author, *Primal: A Quest for the
Lost Soul of Christianity*

Whenever Len Sweet writes something, I am challenged and learn so incredibly much. Whenever Frank Viola writes something, I am challenged and learn so incredibly much. So with both Len and Frank writing together here, you are reading an exponential Jesus-focused challenge and learning experience. They write not just words and sentences, but this is seriously a Spirit-shaped breath of fresh air for the church at large, in all her beautiful and messy forms and shapes, and for Christians of every age and diversity.

— **Dan Kimball**
Author, *They Like Jesus But Not
the Church*

The unrelenting purpose of the Holy Spirit is to lead us into the living presence of Jesus Christ. If we follow the Spirit, Christ can become as real to us as the world was when we were sinners. *Jesus Manifesto* is a compass pointing toward this holy pursuit.

— **Francis Frangipane**
Pastor and Author, *And I Will Be
Found By You*

Amid the many voices calling the church to the work of justice, Leonard Sweet and Frank Viola call us first to Jesus from which all justice flows. Together they help us see how the vision of Christ's supremacy makes possible any and all faithful engagement with the world. There are times when a profound and significant truth needs to be said simply. The *Jesus Manifesto* does just that with an intensity appropriate to the message! I applaud it, and I recommend it.

— **David Fitch**
Author, Pastor, Professor
Northern Seminary

Evangelicals have tended to focus on the work of Christ to the exclusion of valuing the life and model of Jesus as archetypal Christian. By helping us realign ourselves around the magnificent Person at the heart of our faith, this book goes a long way toward correcting that imbalance. Devout, intelligent, challenging, Len and Frank deliver. I sign the manifesto!

— **Alan Hirsch**
Author, *ReJesus: A Wild Messiah
for a Missional Church* and
*Untamed: Reactivating a
Missional Form of Discipleship*

Jesus Manifesto is a priceless treasury revealing the riches of Christ in unique depths yet written with simple language. Prophetic and poignant, Sweet and Viola's words soar high as they glorify the greatest Person in the universe—our Jesus Christ.

— **Anne Jackson**
Speaker and Author, *Permission to Speak Freely: Essays and Art on Fear, Confession, and Grace*

Do you ever feel that "Jesus has left the building"? The Christian religion promises so much in terms of power, forgiveness, joy, and intimacy, but sometimes it feels that those promises are just words. Leonard Sweet and Frank Viola have a radical and Biblical solution, to wit, Jesus. Read this book and you'll find your heart "strangely warmed." That warmth is Him . . . Jesus. This book could change your life and the lives of everyone who cares about the church. I rise up and call the authors blessed!

— **Steve Brown**
Seminary Professor, Reformed Theological Seminary, Orlando, FL;
Author; Host of the syndicated talk show *Steve Brown, Etc.*

The beauty of this book is that it not only deals with the identity of Christ, but the ways that we are made to relate to this Living and Liberating King. I will be buying this book by the caseload to invite others to contemplate the question that has the power to change everything.

— **Chris Seay**
Pastor, Ecclesia Houston
Author, *The Gospel According to Lost* and *The Gospel According to Jesus*
President, Ecclesia Bible Society

From now on my friend Frank Viola will not be known solely by his proposals regarding the church. Len Sweet, my teacher, will not merely be known as a brilliant and original professor. With the writing of *Jesus Manifesto*, they will now be known as followers, broadcasters, ambassadors, and articulators of Jesus. There is no higher role in life. I can offer no higher compliment. Best yet, this role can be taken on by us all: doctors and nurses, policewomen and firemen, teachers and counselors—you name it. In the *Jesus Manifesto* there is room for everyone.

— **Todd Hunter**
Author, *Christianity Beyond Belief*
and *Giving Church Another
Chance*
Anglican Bishop

As we move further into the 21st century, it is becoming evident that there are many voices rising with the intent of redefining the "real Jesus" of the Gospel. Yet these voices reveal a "real Jesus" that is far less the Jesus of Scripture and far more a Jesus made in their image and in their likeness. What is needed in this hour is a clear, compelling, and uncompromised declaration that Jesus is more than a spiritual guide, more than a sacrificial leader, more than one of many "ways" to God. He is indeed the Supreme Ruler of All Creation, and He is Lord of All. As many are defecting the ranks of the faithful for a gospel of their own making, we are indebted to Leonard Sweet and Frank Viola for unhesitatingly issuing a call for the recovery of the true testimony of Scripture, that Jesus indeed is Sovereign Lord, and that He reigns supreme over all the universe, and there is no other God but Him.

— **Mark J. Chironna, M.A. Ph.D.**
The Master's Touch International
Church
Orlando, Florida

In a day when much of Christianity seems to have missed the main point of our faith, *Jesus Manifesto* brings us back to center. Sweet and Viola have given us a matchless presentation of Jesus—one that combines poetic artistry, gripping metaphor, and profound insight. The book masterfully reflects what the Spirit is saying to the church today.

— **Dr. Kenneth C. Ulmer**
President, The King's College
and Seminary
Los Angeles, CA

Like the passionate preachers I grew up hearing at revival meetings, Sweet and Viola point us to Jesus, only Jesus. In a time when the church has such ready access to so many strategies to "change the world" and "make a difference," here is an invitation to return to the heart of evangelical faith—the conviction that God has already given us all we need in Jesus Christ.

— **Jonathan Wilson-Hartgove**
Author, *God's Economy* and *The Wisdom of Stability*

If the Christian church is to fulfill its missional vocation in the world, its life and witness must be bound at every point to the self-revelation of God in Jesus Christ, who is the Way, the Truth, and the Life. While this certainly means wrestling with perennial questions concerning the person and work of Jesus, it also means taking ourselves less seriously and remembering that the answers we give to these questions are not the foundation on which the church stands or falls. In this book Sweet and Viola powerfully remind us that the gospel is not ultimately about doctrines, methods, and programs, but the living presence of Jesus Christ. In calling on Christians of all traditions to refocus our attention on the supremacy of Jesus Christ they have provided a clarion call to the most central aspect of faithful witness—He must become greater and we must become less.

— **John R. Franke**
Clemens Professor of Missional Theology, Biblical Seminary
Author, *Manifold Witness: The Plurality of Truth*

This little book is a fresh and elegant portrayal of Jesus Christ that's epic and timely. It puts a pulse on the main problem in the church today and uniquely stirs both heart and head as it points us to the only solution, Jesus.

— **Pastor Tommy Barnett**
Phoenix First Assembly
Dream Centers: Phoenix, LA, NY

Gandhi once said, "Your Christians are so unlike your Christ." Maybe if we actually knew Christ, we would reflect Him more. Sweet and Viola's *Jesus Manifesto* is the quintessential reintroduction.

— **Sally Morgenthaler**
Worship Evangelism

Wow! What a message, what a word, what a masterful work. My friends Leonard Sweet and Frank Viola have again challenged us to think deeper and go higher in our commitment to the call to genuine and authentic Christian ministry. *Jesus Manifesto: Restoring the Supremacy and Sovereignty of Jesus Christ* is a must read for all serious students, teachers, and leaders in the Lord's church. In this post-modern, high-tech age, where we talk on iPhones, listen to iPods, and write on iPads, but have lost the power of the great "I Am," we are called through this book to come back home—to indeed return to our first love. I believe that this book will cause more than a ripple in the body of Christ.

— **Bishop Donald Hillard, Jr.**
Senior Pastor, Cathedral
International
Presiding Prelate, Covenant
Ecumenical Fellowship and
Cathedral Assemblies

While I may not agree with every detail, the central thrust of this book is vitally important. Its reminder about Christ living in us and seeing our identity in Him is marvelous, as is its recognition that the historical Jesus of the Gospels is the Christ we worship. I fear that liberals (and often conservatives!) read Christ too much through the lens of their culture. Many conservatives read Christ too much through the lens of their church's tradition. Some Pentecostals and charismatics (whose Pentecostal spiritual experience I share) subordinate Christ to their own experience (or traditions developed from others' experiences). But we all need to return to Jesus as our Lord, as this book emphatically reminds us.

— **Craig Keener**
Professor of New Testament,
Palmer Seminary, Eastern
University
Author, *The IVP Bible Background
Commentary*

JESUS
MANIFESTO

JESUS
MANIFESTO

RESTORING THE SUPREMACY AND SOVEREIGNTY OF JESUS CHRIST

LEONARD SWEET AND FRANK VIOLA

THOMAS NELSON
Since 1798

NASHVILLE   DALLAS   MEXICO CITY   RIO DE JANEIRO

Published in Nashville, Tennessee, by Thomas Nelson. Thomas Nelson is a registered trademark of Thomas Nelson, Inc.

Leonard Sweet is published in association with the literary agency of Mark Sweeney & Associates, Bonita Springs, Florida 34135.

Frank Viola is published in association with the literary agency of Daniel Literary Group, Nashville, Tennessee 37215.

Thomas Nelson, Inc., titles may be purchased in bulk for educational, business, fund-raising, or sales promotional use. For information, please e-mail SpecialMarkets@ThomasNelson.com.

Library of Congress Cataloging-in-Publication Data

Sweet, Leonard I.
    Jesus manifesto : Restoring the supremacy and sovereignty of Jesus Christ / Leonard Sweet and Frank Viola.
      p. cm.
    Includes bibliographical references.
    ISBN 978-0-8499-4601-1 (hardcover)
    1. Christian life. I. Viola, Frank. II. Title.
BV4501.3.S9435 2010
248.4—dc22   2010005667

Printed in the United States of America

10 11 12 13 14 WC 7 6 5 4

CONTENTS

122169

Christ will even now, as always, be exalted.

—Philippians 1:20 NASB

INTRODUCTION

"Who Do You Say That I Am?"

The body of Christ is at a crossroads right now. The two common alternatives are to move either to the left or the right. It's our observation, however, that we are living in a unique time, when people are frozen as they look in either of those directions. When they look to the left, they decide that they cannot venture there. When they look to the right, they feel the same.

Whether they realize it or not, people are looking for a fresh alternative—a *third way*. The crossroads today, we believe, is one of moving forward or backward.

What we will present in this book, therefore, is razor-sharp, cut-glass clarity of the Lord Jesus Christ as the Alpha and the

Omega. We will show that *He* is that third way—and the only way—that we can forge a secure path into the future. If the church does not reorient and become Christological at its core, any steps taken will be backwards.

We are aware, of course, that we are swimming upstream in writing a book exclusively about Jesus. It used to be that people had a problem seeing the human in Christ. That sidelined any need to talk about "incarnation." Now it seems that more people have trouble seeing the divine in Christ. This sidelines the need for any "Christology." And beyond both, the reality and experience of an indwelling Lord has been almost lost to the Christian faith.

The Lord Jesus Christ is far beyond what most of us could ever dream or imagine. His greatness, His beauty, and His splendor are unknown to many Christians today. This is why a fresh look at Him—a fresh Christology—is so vital. To put it in a sentence: To faithfully represent Jesus in our time requires re-presenting Him. And that's what we are attempting to do in this book.

We believe that if people will catch hold of the vision that's contained herein, they will find the confidence needed to face an uncertain future.

The book you hold in your hands provides an alternative path that is neither left nor right, but forward. It will lead you to exploration rather than fortification. It is our conviction that we can only cut a path to such future exploration when we take Christ as our All, our "North Star" or "Southern Cross."

As we will argue, the holy Scriptures serve as our road map, or compass, pointing us toward the person of Jesus in all of His riches and depths. So this volume is a means to an end, the end being Christ.

Put another way, Jesus is God's perfect pitch—the divine tuning fork to the eternal.

Every tuning fork needs to be struck to be heard. The striking of the eternal, unchanging tuning fork of heaven took place when a young virgin gave birth to God's only Son in an obscure village in first-century Israel. It struck again on a never-forgotten Friday, with the pounding of six-inch nails. The fork struck a third time—on the third day—when a meek and lowly Nazarene split a tomb wide open and came forth in resurrection life.

Heaven's tuning fork continues to strike today. But whenever we Christians fail to hear it, we lose our way.

JESUS DEFICIT DISORDER

Christians have made the gospel about so many things—things other than Christ. But Jesus Christ is the gravitational pull that brings everything together and gives it meaning. Without Him, all things lose their value. They are but detached pieces floating around in space. *That includes your life.*[1]

It is all too possible to emphasize a spiritual truth, value, virtue, or gift, yet miss Christ, who is Himself the embodiment and incarnation of all of these things.

Seek Christ, embrace Christ, know Christ, and you will have touched Him who is Life. And in Him resides all truth, values, virtues, and gifts, in living color. Beauty has its meaning in the beauty of Christ. Only in Him do we find all that makes us lovely and lovable.

Consider those things that you find arrestingly beautiful in the earth, whether they be beaches, mountains, canyons, or that which lies beneath the ocean. Consider the beauty found in art, music, nature, and the like. Ponder those things in life that you admire and that cause awe and wonder to stir in your soul.

Those things are but images of Jesus Christ, for He is the essence of true beauty.

So what is Christianity? It is Christ. Nothing more. Nothing less. Christianity is not an ideology or a philosophy. Neither is it a new type of morality, social ethic, or worldview. Christianity is the "good news" that beauty, truth, and goodness are found in a person. And true humanity and community are founded on and experienced by connection to that person.

Conversion is more than a change in *direction*; it's a change in *connection*. The Bible's use of the ancient Hebrew word *shubh* to call for "repentance"—in Deuteronomy 4:30 and Nehemiah 1:9, for example—implies not viewing God from a distance but entering into a relationship where God is command central of the human connection.

In that regard, we feel a massive disconnect in the church today, and we believe that the major disease of today's church is JDD: Jesus Deficit Disorder. The person of Jesus has become increasingly politically incorrect and is being replaced by the language of "justice," "morality," "values," and "leadership principles." The world likes Jesus; they just don't like the church. But increasingly, the church likes the church, yet it doesn't like Jesus.

Something is wrong when it's easier for some Christians to think of the world without Christ than the world without Bach or the Beatles or Bono. When we dethrone Jesus Christ from His rightful place, we tarnish the face of Christianity and redefine it out of existence.

Can our problems really be caused by something so basic and simple as losing sight of Christ? We believe the answer is a resounding *Yes*. Answers other than Christ to the problems of the church today mean that we are more into solvents than solutions. For that reason, this global, Google world needs a meta-narrative more than ever, and the Jesus Story is the interpreting system of all other systems. In this hour, the testimony that we feel God has called us to bear revolves around the primacy of the Lord Jesus Christ. Specifically, we need to decide how we are going to answer one question.

THE ULTIMATE QUESTION

"Who do *you say* that I am?"[2] is the question required of every generation, and every generation must answer it for itself.

The historic Christian creeds are an expression of the need to answer Jesus' "Who do *you say* that I am?" question. But that "you say" is contextual. Each new generation, in every culture, is given a "you say." And if we get our "you say" wrong, we get everything wrong, since Jesus is Alpha and Omega, the beginning and the end of all things.

Every revival and restoration in the church has been a rediscovery of some aspect of Christ in the process of answering this critical question. In fact, three features are present in every awakening in the history of the Christian church: (1) a rediscovery of the "living Word," or the Scriptures and its authority; (2) a rediscovery of the living Christ and His supremacy; and (3) a rediscovery of the living Spirit and the Spirit's gifts and power to manifest Christ in the context of that culture. God has a history of taking seriously people who take the eternal Word seriously.

Jesus Himself said that when He is lifted up, *He will draw* all people to Himself.[3] But because we don't trust Jesus to do what He says He will do, or believe that He is who He says He is, or have not caught a glimpse of His infinite glory, we sit at drawing boards and draw up programs and methods and draft strategies that we hope might bring people to Christ. But Jesus could not have been clearer: the only begotten Son of God[4] *is* the draw. Our mission is simply to lift Him up in a context that our culture can understand and appreciate. Whenever this happens, the rest will take care of itself.

Unfortunately, "Who do you say that I am?" is no longer the only question. "What are you doing to bring in the kingdom of God?" is now an equally asked question, as is "What are you doing for justice?" and "In what causes are you engaged?" Or "What are you doing to evangelize the world?" and "To whom are you accountable?" and "What's your gift?" And especially, "What kind of a leader are you?"

Yet Jesus quizzed Peter with one ultimate question, and only one.[5] And that one decisive question is the same one He asks us today.

It is not, "Are you ready to accept leadership status in My church?"

It is not, "Do you know how to build a movement?"

It is not, "How many people did you lead to Me?"

It is not, "Have you spoken in tongues yet?"

It is not, "Is leadership your passion?"

It is not, "To whom will you be accountable?"

It is not, "Are you doing better than the best you can do so God will be happy with you?"

And it is not, "Will you surround yourself with people who have leadership potential and will make you look good?"

The question is only this: *"Do you love Me?"*

What does Jesus want from us? Leadership? Or love? Unfortunately, we cannot properly love Him if we haven't caught sight of how incredibly glorious He is. But once we do—once we catch a sighting of Jesus Christ in all His glory—we will gladly exchange our dusty rites, Christian-speak, and pop-culture church-building tactics for the joy of becoming a walking, breathing "Jesus Manifesto."

A LIVING MANIFESTO

In the following pages, we hope to bring your vision and understanding of Jesus Christ into sharper focus. We hope to present our Lord to you in such a way that you cannot help but love Him, that you cannot help but fall at His feet and give Him your undying devotion—not out of guilt, duty, obligation, or fear, but because your heart has been captured by a glimpse of the greatest person this world has ever known, Jesus the Christ. Out of such love flows everything else.

In contrast, we do not echo or condone the cheap, happy-clappy "Jesus talk" that so often creeps into religious conversations today. We believe that there are many ways to take Jesus' name "in vain,"[6] and one of them is by invoking the name of Jesus without really knowing Him. How embarrassed our Lord must be in hearing His name used as some sort of amulet, magic spell, or religious slogan.

Die Lösung des Rätsels des Lebens in Raum und Zeit liegt ausserhalb von Raum un Zeit.

The solution of the riddle of life in space and time lies outside space and time.

—Ludwig Wittgenstein[7]

We have purposely written this book in an ancient devotional tone—one that we feel is lacking in the church today. By it, we wish to show the difference between invoking the name of Jesus in vain and using His name in a way that reveals His beauty and honors His person. In short, we believe that Jesus has gotten shortchanged today, and we would like to see that trend reversed.

Ω

At the end of their lives, some of the world's greatest thinkers often arrived at a simplicity that escaped them at the beginning of their careers. For example, Ludwig Wittgenstein, who many believe was the greatest philosopher of the twentieth century, crowned a lifetime of thought with the discovery of the "duck-rabbit,"[8] the reversible image that faces one way as a duck and the other way as a rabbit. Wittgenstein felt that this one cartoonish image, which proved that something could not be both a duck and a rabbit at the same time (or more precisely, could not be "seen as" such), conveyed more about truth than his greatest philosophical writings.[9]

Karl Barth, whom some consider to be the greatest theologian of the twentieth century, was asked to summarize his twelve volumes on church dogmatics. He answered by repeating a line from an old children's hymn: "Jesus loves me, this I know, for the Bible tells me so."[10]

Today, the church needs a conversion to its forgotten "first love": "Jesus loves me, this I know."[11] The most theologically precise affirmation of Christian faith in the Bible is the shorthand creed of this *Jesus Manifesto*, taken from 1 John 4:16: "We believe in the love God has for us."[12] It is a love that came not in the form of abstract principle but of an actual person, the very Son of God.

Note John's words in 1 John 4:19: "We love Him because He first loved us."

But how are we to *live our lives* as followers of Christ? Sandwiched between these two verses is the answer: "As He [Jesus] is, so are we in this world."[13] The Bible doesn't *just* promise us "eternal life"[14]; it also offers us the gift of life lived through Christ.[15] Has the popularity of one verse of Scripture—John 3:16—and its emphasis on "eternal life" in the future blinded us to what the Bible has to say about life in the now?

You and I are meant to be *living* epistles—that is, "Jesus Manifestos"—in our world. Cities set on a hill. Salt and light.[16] That's why we wrote this book.

Thomas Aquinas, whom many consider to be the church's greatest teacher and philosopher, wrote that his *Summa Theologica*[17] was nothing but straw, since no words could begin to convey the radiant mystery of the divine. Similarly, this book, even though its subject is the King of kings and Lord of lords,[18] is only dry straw. Nonetheless, we hope it will birth in your life a new burst of wonder and insight into the earthly, the exalted, and the indwelling Jesus. But even more, we hope that you will be compelled to respond to the love He has so graciously poured out upon you—and become a Jesus Manifesto in your own community.

LEONARD SWEET AND FRANK VIOLA

CHAPTER 1

THE OCCUPATION OF ALL THINGS

The center and the circumference of the Christian life is none other than the person of Christ. All other things, including those related to Him, are eclipsed by the sight of His peerless worth. God put an image in our galaxy to demonstrate what Christ is to us. We call it the sun. Without it, no life can exist on planet Earth. We are dependent upon the sun for everything. And just as the sun is the center of our solar system, Jesus Christ is the centerpiece of God's universe, and even our lives.

> To you who fear My name the Sun of Righteousness shall arise with healing in His wings.
>
> —Malachi 4:2[1]

As Dietrich Bonhoeffer pointed out in his seminal book, *Christ the Center* (German text, 1960), Jesus is the center of human existence, of history, and the center between God and nature.[2] History is *His* story. Of this connection, British author H. G. Wells remarked, "I am a historian, I am not a believer, but I must confess as a historian that this penniless preacher from Nazareth is irrevocably the very center of history. Jesus Christ is easily the most dominant figure in all history."[3]

Yet Christ isn't just found in the center. He's also found in the corners and on the edges, just as the light of the sun hits all of planet Earth. Indeed, Jesus is not just the Lord of the middle and the margins; He's the God of the whole show. The Bright and Morning Star[4] gives light to all that exists.

After two thousand years, Jesus' light shines ever brighter, and we can track His brilliant gleam into the shadowy realms of whatever gloom there is. Knowing Christ profoundly and in reality is the chief pursuit of the Christian life. The Lord is preeminently concerned about our knowing Him.[5] We are "called into the fellowship of [God's] Son."[6]

> Lead, kindly light, amid th' encircling gloom.
> —John Henry Newman (1801–1890)[7]

God is not so much about fixing things that have gone wrong in our lives as He is about finding us in our brokenness and giving us Christ. When Christ is not central and supreme in our lives, everything about life shifts out of orbit and moves out of kilter. So for Christians, our first task is to know Jesus. And out of that knowing, we will come to love Him, adore Him, proclaim Him, and manifest Him.

THE OCCUPATION OF THE HEAVENS

The entire heavenly realm—the Father, the Holy Spirit, and the angelic hosts—are occupied with Christ. The second member of the Trinity is no second thought of God, but His very forethought and first thought. There are only a few places in the Gospels where we find God the Father speaking audibly, and in each case, He points to His Son:

> And suddenly a voice came from heaven, saying, "This is My beloved Son, in whom I am well pleased."[8]

> While he was still speaking, behold, a bright cloud overshadowed them; and suddenly a voice came out of the cloud, saying, "This is My beloved Son, in whom I am well pleased. Hear Him!"[9]

Jesus once said, "Out of the abundance of the heart the mouth speaks."[10] Whenever God the Father speaks, He speaks of His Son, for Christ is foremost on His heart. The Bread of Life can be tasted in "every word that proceeds from the mouth of God."[11] In fact, when God expresses Himself, it is Christ. We can rightly say that God spoke Himself into human life in the person of the Lord Jesus. For this reason, John called Christ *the logos*, the living Word of God.[12] God's Word is a *person*. The one true God has revealed Himself completely and finally in Jesus: "No one has ever seen God. But the unique One, who is himself God, is near to the Father's heart. He has revealed God to us."[13]

In like manner, the Holy Spirit, the great Revelator, also reveals Christ. And Christ is the only *thing* that the Spirit reveals. He has no other revelation. The Spirit introduces Jesus, usually in some new way.[14]

But when the Helper comes, whom I shall send to you from the Father, the Spirit of truth who proceeds from the Father, He will testify of Me.[15]

However, when He, the Spirit of truth, has come, He will guide you into all truth; for He will not speak on His own authority, but whatever He hears He will speak; and He will tell you things to come. He will glorify Me, for He will take of what is Mine and declare it to you. All things that the Father has are Mine. Therefore I said that He will take of Mine and declare it to you.[16]

Someone may object by saying, "But Jesus said that the Holy Spirit would reprove the world of sin, righteousness, and judgment." This is true. But Jesus makes Himself the reference point for these things.[17] Therefore, the question becomes: How does the Spirit convict the world?

He does it by showing Christ to the world.[18] The Holy Spirit has come to reveal, to glorify, to magnify, to unveil, to *exalt* the Lord Jesus Christ. He takes what is true of Christ and makes it real and alive in the lives of human beings. That's the occupation and preoccupation of the Spirit. It's what He does for a living.

But there's something more. The Father was so consumed with Christ that He was pleased to place all the divine fullness into Him:

For in Him dwells all the fullness of the Godhead bodily.[19]

For it pleased the Father that in Him all the fullness should dwell.[20]

Finally, all of the angelic hosts live to worship and serve the Lord Jesus. They, too, are occupied with Christ: Hebrews 1:6 says,

> When [God] again brings the firstborn into the world, He says: "Let all the angels of God worship Him."[21]

In a word, Jesus is heaven's passion and occupation.

THE OCCUPATION OF CREATION

Paul tells us that the entire universe was created by Christ, through Christ, and for Christ. In addition, all things in heaven and earth are held together in Christ and will one day be summed up in Him. Consequently, creation is also occupied with Christ.

> For by Him all things were created that are in heaven and that are on earth, visible and invisible, whether thrones or dominions or principalities or powers. All things were created through Him and for Him. And He is before all things, and in Him all things consist.[22]

> That in the dispensation of the fullness of the times He might gather together in one all things in Christ, both which are in heaven and which are on earth—in Him.[23]

If you explore the seven days of Creation in light of the New Testament, you will discover that everything in the visible creation is an image of Jesus. For example:

Christ is light.[24]

Christ is water.[25]

Christ is the life that emerged on the third day after the
waters below the firmament were separated from the
waters above.[26]

Christ is the true Vine.[27]

Christ is wheat and the bread of life.[28]

Christ is the sun,[29] the moon,[30] and the morning star.[31]

Christ is the true Lamb.[32]

Christ is the model man.[33]

Christ is the real Sabbath.[34]

The Lord Jesus is written in the bloodstream of the universe. The
Creator left an impression of Christ in everything. That which
came forth from the lungs of God when the worlds were spoken
into existence was Jesus. The entire cosmos bears His magnificent
imprint.

In a matchless metaphor, Tertullian wrote that Christ (*Logos*)
pervades the world in the same way as honey in the comb. This
shouldn't surprise us, since the whole created order was created
by, in, through, and for Christ. And the whole creation groans
for Jesus to deliver it from the bondage of corruption and fill it
with His infinite sweetness.[35]

The Tree of Life

The tree of life my soul hath seen,
laden with fruit and always green.

The trees of nature, fruitless be
compared with Christ the apple tree.

His beauty doth all things excel.
By faith I know but ne'er can tell
the glory which I now can see,
in Jesus Christ the apple tree.

For happiness I long have sought,
and pleasure dearly I have bought.
I miss'd for all—but now I see—
'tis found in Jesus Christ the apple tree.

I'm weary with my former toil.
Here I will sit and rest awhile.
Under the shadow I will be
of Jesus Christ the apple tree.

I'll sit and eat this truth divine.
It cheers my heart like spirit'al wine;
And now this fruit is sweet to me,
that grows on Christ the apple tree.

This fruit does make my soul to thrive.
It keeps my dying faith alive,
which makes my soul in haste to be
with Jesus Christ the apple tree.

—Eighteenth-century Christmas carol[36]

THE OCCUPATION OF THE OLD TESTAMENT

And what of the holy Scriptures? Jesus Himself answered this question, declaring that the Hebrew Scriptures are also occupied with Him:

> You search the Scriptures because you think they give you eternal life. But the Scriptures point to me![37]

> And beginning with Moses and all the Prophets, he explained to them what was said in all the Scriptures concerning himself. . . . Then their eyes were opened and they recognized him.[38]

> He said to them, "This is what I told you while I was still with you: Everything must be fulfilled that is written about me in the Law of Moses, the Prophets and the Psalms." Then he opened their minds so they could understand the Scriptures.[39]

Jesus Christ makes Scripture intelligible. He is the key that unlocks the entire biblical canon. When one reads the New Testament carefully, this becomes evident. For instance, the entire story of Israel is the story of the Messiah, Jesus. Christ is the new Israel, the new Jacob.

> . . . and was there until the death of Herod, that it might be fulfilled which was spoken by the Lord by the prophet, saying, "Out of Egypt I called My Son."[40]

Now to Abraham and his Seed were the promises made. He does not say, "And to seeds," as of many, but as of one, "And to your Seed," who is Christit.[41]

Jacob had twelve sons, who became the twelve tribes of Israel. Jesus also chose twelve disciples to follow Him.

Israel was tempted in the wilderness for forty years. Jesus was tempted in the wilderness for forty days. In fact, the same temptations that Israel experienced in the wilderness were repeated when Christ was in the wilderness. To combat them, Jesus quoted the words of Moses to satan. Interestingly, they were the exact same words that Moses gave to Israel when she was tempted.[42]

The book of Genesis further demonstrates the Scriptures' preoccupation with Christ. Chapters 1 and 2 were never intended to be the battleground for the Creation-versus-evolution debate. They are rather an unveiling of Christ and His church. Jesus is the new Adam. The church is the new Eve. And the gospel of John is the new Genesis (compare Genesis 1–2 with John 1–2).[43]

Death reigned from Adam to Moses, even over those who had not sinned according to the likeness of the transgression of Adam, who is a type of Him who was to come.[44]

And so it is written, "The first man Adam became a living being." The last Adam became a life-giving spirit. . . . The first man was of the earth, made of dust; the second Man is the Lord from heaven.[45]

"For this reason a man shall leave his father and mother and be joined to his wife, and the two shall become one flesh." This is a great mystery, but I speak concerning Christ and the church.[46]

Have you ever noticed how the New Testament writers quoted the Hebrew Scriptures? Go back to the Old Testament and read the quoted texts. You'll learn that the New Testament writers were using a method of interpretation that would drive most textual critics insane. It isn't at all modern. It's as if they were reading the texts out of context.

But they weren't. They were reading it through the lens of Christ. For example, consider Colossians 2:16–17: "Let no one judge you in food or in drink, or regarding a festival or a new moon or sabbaths, which are a shadow of things to come, but *the substance is of Christ.*"[47]

Consider the way Jesus Himself interpreted the Scriptures in light of Himself. Then combine that with the way the Gospel authors, Paul of Tarsus, and the writer of Hebrews saw Christ in the Hebrew Scriptures.[48] By doing so, you'll be furnished with a new lens through which to read your Old Testament. Christ will leap off of almost every page. When viewed through the template of Jesus Christ, the Old Testament becomes a living piece of art. It gets transformed into God's picture book showing us the wonders of Jesus.[49]

As John Calvin once said, "We ought to read the Scriptures with the express design of finding Christ in them. Whoever shall turn aside from this object, though he may weary himself throughout his whole life in learning, will never attain the knowledge of the truth; for what wisdom can we have without the wisdom of God?"[50]

Charles Spurgeon underscored this point, saying, "For every text in Scripture, there is a road to the metropolis of the Scriptures, that is Christ. And my dear brother, your business is, when you get to a text, to say, 'Now what is the road to Christ?' . . . I have never yet found a text that had not got a road to Christ in it."[51]

Note that we aren't expecting religious Jews to see Jesus in the Old Testament, although we wish they would. But it doesn't violate the Jewish faith if they do not. However, it does violate the Christian faith if we do not see Jesus in the Old Testament. Either the Hebrew Bible is a part of the Christian Bible or it isn't.

In short, Christians can only know the full meaning of the Old Testament by looking at the end of the story, which has dawned in Christ. The beginning cannot be understood apart from the end. Genesis cannot be fully understood without Revelation. We, therefore, should understand the Old Testament Scriptures in light of Jesus Christ. He is the Rosetta Stone of the Bible.

THE OCCUPATION OF THE NEW TESTAMENT

The New Testament is also occupied with Christ. It goes without saying that Jesus is the subject of the four Gospels. Their pages are dominated by His amazing life, the horrors of His crucifixion, and the wonders of His resurrection.

In the book of Acts, Jesus—who is now ascended—extends His presence through His body, the church. Luke opened Acts by saying that his Gospel write-up (the gospel of Luke) was a record of "all that Jesus *began* both to do and teach" (emphasis added). The book of Acts is the *continuation* of what Jesus did and taught through His body.

The apostles' message throughout Acts is not the plan of salvation. It's not a theology or a set of doctrines either. It is a person—Christ:

> . . . and that He may send Jesus Christ, who was preached to you before.[52]

> Then Philip went down to the city of Samaria and preached Christ unto them.[53]

> Immediately he preached the Christ in the synagogues, that He is the Son of God.[54]

In Acts 2:42, we read about something called "the apostles' doctrine." Following the day of Pentecost, the church in Jerusalem continued steadfastly in this teaching. But what exactly was it?

Before we answer that question, let's reframe it. Here's the scene. The Twelve have just baptized three thousand new converts. Tomorrow, they will begin teaching these new converts. *What will they teach them?*

Look across the landscape of contemporary Christianity and ask yourself what many of today's preachers would teach them. Here are some certain answers. They would teach them about . . .

- how to live a good, clean life
- church multiplication strategies
- the mark of the beast and end-times prophecy
- the 613 laws of Moses, exhorting them to obey each one of them

- the 614th commandment: "Thou shalt not forget"
- the visions and dreams in Daniel and Ezekiel
- signs, wonders, and miracles
- how to build a movement
- divine healing
- how to live by faith
- how to save the lost
- Creation versus evolution
- leadership principles
- how to memorize the Scriptures
- social justice
- prosperity
- the believer's right to "name it and claim it"
- spiritual warfare
- how to observe Israel's feasts
- wealth and health
- systematic theology

Now compare this list with what the apostles actually taught the early believers. John, one of the Twelve, told us plainly:

> That which was from the beginning, which we have heard, which we have seen with our eyes, which we have looked upon, and our hands have handled, concerning the Word of life—the life was manifested, and we have seen, and bear witness, and declare to you that eternal life which was with the Father and was manifested to us—that which we have seen and heard we declare to you, that you also may have fellowship with us; and truly our fellowship is with the Father and with His Son Jesus Christ.[55]

The apostles' teaching was Jesus Christ:

> And daily in the temple, and in every house, they ceased not to teach and preach Jesus Christ.[56]

> God's presence is not accidental in relation to his teaching, but is essential to it. God's presence in human form, in the humble form of a servant, is itself the teaching.
>
> —Sören Kierkegaard[57]

The Twelve lived with the Son of God for almost four years. They watched Him sleep, eat, heal the sick, cast out demons, comfort the afflicted, and afflict the comfortable. But more importantly, in living color they beheld the taproot and headwaters of Jesus' incredible life. *They watched Him fellowship with His Father.*

In short, the New Testament writers were completely consumed with Christ. He was their message, their teaching, their proclamation, their very life. And everything else flowed out of intimate fellowship with Him.

THE MESSAGE AND MINISTRY OF PAUL OF TARSUS

Both of us have developed the habit of counting the number of times we hear preachers mention the Lord Jesus in their talks.[58] Sadly, in many cases, contemporary preachers and teachers who spend an hour speaking on a subject mention the Lord just once or twice. Sometimes the number of mentions is zero. Compare that with how many times Paul referred to Christ in the opening chapters of some of his letters:

Colossians 1 (29 verses): 30 references to Christ

Ephesians 1 (23 verses): 26 references

Philippians 1 (30 verses): 20 references

Romans 1:1–9: 11 references

1 Corinthians 1:1–10: 13 references

2 Corinthians 1:1–5: 5 references

Galatians 1:1–4: 4 references

If you were to count the total number of times Paul spoke of Christ in each epistle, it would blow your mind. The same is true for the other New Testament authors.

Note that Paul wrote most of the New Testament Epistles and planted most of the Gentile churches in the first century. His incessant mention of the Lord Jesus speaks volumes. ("Out of the abundance of the heart the mouth speaks."[59]) Paul was consumed with his crucified, risen, and reigning Lord. If the heart is occupied with Christ, Jesus will pour forth from the lips and the pen. He will ooze out of every pore.

In a nutshell, New Testament ministry is the ministry of Jesus Christ:

> To me, who am less than the least of all the saints, this grace was given, that I should preach among the Gentiles the unsearchable riches of Christ.[60]

> We proclaim Him, admonishing every man and teaching every man with all wisdom, so that we may present every man complete in Christ.[61]

. . . that I might preach [Christ] among the Gentiles.[62]

For we do not preach ourselves, but Christ Jesus the Lord.[63]

Since the Scriptures are inspired by the Father and the Holy Spirit, it stands to reason that each word of holy Writ would breathe a revelation of the Lord Jesus Christ. God the Father is consumed with His Son, and so is the Spirit.

In sum, the Father, the Holy Spirit, the angels, all of creation, the Scriptures, and the early apostles' ministries all point their fingers to Jesus. The spotlight of heaven and earth never leaves Christ. He is the melody, the harmony, the rhythm, the tempo, and the music behind all things. The heavens and the earth sing His song and play His tune.

PRACTICAL IMPLICATIONS

We are keenly sensitive to how hard it may be for some reading this chapter to hear such an elevation of Jesus Christ. We hope you will stay with us a little longer. We have written this book to be more of a dance than a talk about dancing.

We are also aware that some reading this chapter may blithely nod in agreement, but without realizing the staggering implications of what's just been presented. We know because we've both said what we're saying here before, and some people shoot past it as they would skip over a commercial.

So what does this mean practically?

It means that if a person is truly inspired by the Spirit of God when he or she is speaking, that individual's message will be Christ.

Jesus will bleed through every word. Why? Because the Spirit is totally occupied with Christ.

It also means that when someone is teaching from the Scriptures—and being true to the Word of God—that teacher will unveil Christ through the text. Jesus will be drawn out and lifted up from the pages of the Bible. Why? Because the Scriptures are completely occupied with Christ.

It means that Christ will be on the lips of every person and church who is walking in the Spirit, and He will leap out from their lifestyles.

> The Church's one foundation Is Jesus Christ, her Lord; She is His new creation By water and the Word. From heaven He came and sought her To be His holy bride; With His own blood He bought her, And for her life He died.
>
> —Samuel J. Stone[64]

It means that church members will know their Lord better than they know their church programs.

It means that Jesus will get airplay in their conversations.

It means His melody will resound through their actions and reverberate in their attitudes.

Consequently, those who do not present Christ when they minister not only miss a note, but they play the wrong tune.

The tragedy of our time is that countless preachers, teachers, even healers are giving dozens of sermons, lectures, and messages, relegating Jesus to little more than a footnote or a flourish to some other subject. At best, He gets honorable mention. What is lacking is a groundbreaking revelation of Christ that boggles the mind and enraptures the heart. (More on this later.)

Depending on what Christian tradition you hail from, the word *revelation* may ring spooky or mystical to your ears. But it's really not. The New Testament authors repeatedly used it to describe an unveiling—a spiritual seeing—an inward knowing of Christ. Everything in the Christian life stems from such a revelation of Him. Consider Jesus' own words: "He said to them, 'But who do you say that I am?' Simon Peter answered and said, 'You are the Christ, the Son of the living God.' Jesus answered and said to him, 'Blessed are you, Simon Bar-Jonah, for flesh and blood has not revealed this to you, but My Father who is in heaven.'"[65]

Paul's ministry was built on an inward revelation of Christ:

But when it pleased God, who separated me from my mother's womb and called me through His grace, to reveal His Son in me, that I might preach Him among the Gentiles . . . [66]

Now to Him who is able to establish you according to my gospel and the preaching of Jesus Christ, according to the revelation of the mystery kept secret since the world began . . . [67]

In like manner, Paul's throne-ascending prayer in Ephesians was for the Spirit to reveal Christ to His people: "I have not stopped giving thanks for you, remembering you in my prayers. I keep asking that the God of our Lord Jesus Christ, the glorious Father, may give you the Spirit of wisdom and revelation, so that you may know him better."[68]

Let us press the point: What is it that will change the course of Christianity, putting it back on course? What will emancipate God's people from all the things that Jesus nailed to His cross? What will create a spiritual revolution in the world today? What one thing will satisfy the heart of God and cause us to love Him with an undying passion, making "our hearts burn within us" when we read the Scriptures?[69]

It's not the doctrine of the person of Jesus. It's an inward revelation of Christ to our hearts by the Holy Spirit—a progressive unveiling of the person who stands behind the sacred page and is the occupation of all things. "For it is the God who commanded light to shine out of darkness, who has shone in our hearts to give the light of the knowledge of the glory of God in the face of Jesus Christ."[70]

WHAT'S YOUR OCCUPATION?

So what is your chief occupation in life and ministry? Here's a hint: Whatever you are occupied with comes out of your mouth. It's what you talk about *most* of the time.[71]

For many Christians, their occupation has nothing to do with spiritual things at all. For others who are more inclined to divine matters, their occupation is evangelism. For some, it's church multiplication that matters most. For others, it's memorizing the Bible and learning theology. Many Christians are most occupied with social action, while others are most occupied with leadership and its various principles. Still others are mainly occupied with missions, or praise and worship; the casting out of demons, or healing; miracles, holiness, or the end times; spiritual authority and submission, justice, or politics; and so forth. The list is endless.

But all of these are "its"—just *things*. In fact, the Christian family has swung so far from its Lord that most of our preaching and teaching today is an "it" rather than a "Him."

The result: We focus on "things"—even good and religious

things. And the Lord Jesus Christ is pushed off into a corner. (He usually gets inserted somewhere in the message as a side dish, but He's rarely the main course.)

> The characteristic of Christianity lies in the fact that its source, depth, and riches are involved with the knowledge of God's Son. It matters not how much we know of methods or doctrines or power. What really matters is the knowledge of the Son of God.
>
> —Watchman Nee[72]

Yet, the reality is that Christ trumps everything. All Scripture testifies of Him. The Father exalts Him. The Spirit magnifies Him. The angels worship Him. The early church knew Him as her passion, her message, and the unction of her life. Christ was her specialty. He was her Bridegroom and head. She specialized in nothing else.

All told, there's *nothing* worth pursuing outside of Christ.

To our minds, there is one reason why a Christian would not be absolutely occupied and consumed with Christ. *That person's eyes have not been opened to see His greatness.*

The sad truth is that the Jesus who is preached so often today is so shallow, so small, and so uncaptivating that countless believers are enthralled with countless other things.

A DIVINE CAPTIVITY

The need today is for the scales to fall from our eyes so that we may see the infinite greatness of our Lord. That requires the existence of those who can present Him with astounding power and reality.

This, of course, necessitates that those who have been smitten by Christ themselves impart that same sterling vision of Him to others. As T. Austin-Sparks once put it:

> Divine fullness is only going to be reached by a progressive and ever increasing revelation of Christ and His significance. Such a revelation—unless we misunderstand the record of God's ways from old—comes firstly by an apprehended instrument which is taken into the deeps with God: then it is given forth as His truth to His people: and then it becomes the inwrought experience and knowledge of such as really mean business with God—not as their blessing, but as to His purpose and inheritance in them.[73]

Once our eyes are opened to see the incredible richness and captivating beauty of Jesus, either our other pursuits will take a backseat, or we will discover them anew and afresh "in the light of His glory and grace."[74] Like Paul, we will be "apprehended"— ambushed and arrested by Christ.[75]

This is precisely what happened to one of the greatest minds that the Christian world has ever produced. As we mentioned in the introduction, near the end of his life, the great theologian Thomas Aquinas had a revelation of Jesus Christ. In the afterglow of that revelation, he penned, "I can write no more; compared with what I have seen, all that I have written seems to me as straw."[76]

A spellbinding apprehension of Jesus by our hearts wipes everything else off the table. Jesus bests all things. He dwarfs every competitor. Concisely, a person who is fully occupied with Christ, who knows Him well, and who is in touch with Him through daily fellowship can boldly say, "Christ is all I need. You can strip everything else away from me, and I would still be left with Christ. Take away my gifts and my ministry; take away signs and wonders; take away the sense of His presence; take away my ability to read; and take away every spiritual and religious pursuit I have, and *I will still have Christ*. And in having Him, I have everything."

A PERSON-DRIVEN LIFE

Our plea is that you will bring the Lord Jesus Christ back into view, making Him the lighthouse of your life and giving Him His rightful place of centrality, supremacy, and sovereignty. We implore you: Make Christ the center. Make Him the circumference. And fill in the difference with Him as well.

As you continue to read this book, we pray that the Spirit of God will give you an ever-widening, skyrocketing, heaven-ascending revelation of the Lord Jesus, and that upon receiving such revelation, you will fall in love with Him so that He becomes your complete occupation. We believe that "God has a secret stairway into every heart,"[77] and in this book we have tried to forge as many keys as we can envision to inspire you to take those steps homeward.

> Christ is all (Colossians 3:11). These three words are the essence and substance of Christianity. If our hearts can really go along with them, it is well with our souls; if not, we may be sure we have yet much to learn.
> —J. C. Ryle, Anglican bishop[78]

CHAPTER 2

A BOTTLE IN THE OCEAN

In this book, we are arguing that Christianity is Christ—nothing more, nothing less. Some reading this statement may say, "Of *course* Christianity is all about Jesus. What you're saying is nothing new, and it's not really needed." We wish that were true. But in our experience, it is not.

We have met countless "Bible-believing Christians" who would say, "Yeah, Jesus is Lord and Savior. I got that T-shirt long ago. But we must now mature, go deeper, and go on to *other things*."

Go deeper? And what "other things"? Other things beyond Christ? Is there anything deeper than Christ? This line of thinking reveals the very problem we're seeking to address in this book.

The person who believes that a Christian or a church can graduate beyond Christ has never fully seen the Jesus that Paul of Tarsus preached and declared. Instead, such an individual has a very small Christ, one who's far less than the one who fills the pages of the New Testament.

Consider Paul's words in Philippians, written near the end of his life: "But whatever was to my profit I now consider loss for the sake of Christ. What is more, I consider everything a loss compared to the surpassing greatness of knowing Christ Jesus my Lord, for whose sake I have lost all things. I consider them rubbish, that I may gain Christ."[1]

Look again at those last few words: "I consider them rubbish, that I may gain Christ." An amazing statement. What was it about Jesus that was so incredible, so captivating, and so compelling that it caused a former Pharisee to be totally enamored with Him?

The answer is found in Paul's letter to the Colossians.[2]

ONE INCREDIBLE LETTER

The letter called Colossians is the high-water mark of divine revelation in all the New Testament. Ephesians shares that accolade, and Romans comes in just behind.[3]

Scholars have spent much airtime trying to figure out the exact nature of the teaching that had captured the minds and hearts of the Colossian Christians. Whatever it was, a few things are clear. First, the Colossian church had become distracted from Jesus. They became occupied with other things, even religious things.[4]

Second, the church had dethroned Christ. She was no longer "holding fast to the Head."[5] It appears that some people had come through Colosse, peddling a teaching that moved the church off her center and left her in a sterling mess. Now the Colossians were subjecting Jesus to a lower place. They were no longer living under His sovereignty, and they had lost touch with His supremacy.

What's striking about this letter is that Paul didn't come out of the gate swinging against the false teaching. Instead, he first presented one of the most sublime, unparalleled revelations of the Lord Jesus in all of Scripture. Then, in light of his stunningly rich presentation of Christ, Paul exposed the teaching that was circulating in the church as a philosophy "not according to Christ."[6]

What a unique way to combat error—drown God's people in a revelation of the image of the invisible God, who delivered us from darkness, redeemed us, and made us part of His eternal kingdom.[7]

This alone should cause us to pause in reflection. In times of crisis, the church doesn't need rules established, laws passed, or wolves shot. She needs a seismic revelation of her Lord—the fullness of the Godhead in bodily form.[8]

Sadly, many of us today combat problems and erroneous teachings with laws, rules, religious duty—and the mother of all religious tools: *guilt*. Some preachers need a travel agent to handle all the guilt trips they put on God's people. But there is a big difference between putting a guilt trip on Christians and unveiling Christ to them. When Christ is presented in power, the Spirit of God will undoubtedly convict those who are walking in contradiction to their new nature. But Holy Spirit conviction and man-induced guilt and condemnation are two very different things.

Paul refused to employ any of the tricks of the trade, such as guilt, fear, or strong-armed manipulation. Instead, he gave the Colossian believers a stunningly elegant vision of Christ—exalted, glorious, high and lifted up. To his mind, if he could present Christ in reality, life, and power, it would blow the false teaching to bits. All the problems in the Colossian church would fade into the background. No earthly distraction, whether true or false, could stand up to the glaring light of God's glory in the face of Jesus Christ.

To use a gambling metaphor, Paul bet on Christ and believed that He was enough to win the hearts of the Colossian Christians. Consequently, the apostle sought to put salve on the believers' eyes so they would be able to see the overwhelming greatness of their Lord. The Christ that the Colossians knew was simply too small. That was why they became susceptible to chasing other things—including religious ones—in the first place.

Sound familiar?

Paul's goal was to strip away every distraction that was being held before their eyes and leave them with nothing but Christ. He dared to displace all rules, regulations, laws, and everything else that religion offers, with a person—the Lord Jesus Himself. As far as Paul was concerned, God hadn't sent a Ruler of the rules, a Regulator of the regulations, a Pontiff of the pontifications, or a Principal of the principles. He had sent the very embodiment of divine fullness. So, he reasoned, if the Colossians could just get a glimpse of the glories of Christ, He would be enough. The Spirit would electrify their hearts and restore them to a living relationship with the head of the body. So Paul threw down his trump card—*the Lord Jesus Christ*. He presented a panoramic vision of Jesus that exhausts the minds of mortal men.

INTRODUCING A JESUS MOST OF US HAVE NEVER IMAGINED

In chapter 1, Paul was in full flight. He began his letter by pointing out that if the church would lay hold of Christ and become absorbed with Him, they would bear fruit. They would be filled with the knowledge of God's will. They would receive spiritual understanding and wisdom. They would walk worthy of the Lord and live pleasing in God's sight. They would receive God's infinite power, endurance, patience, and joy. And finally, they would be provoked to thankfulness.

Paul then began to unveil Him. Behold this amazing Christ

in whom we have redemption through His blood, the forgiveness of sins. He is the image of the invisible God, the firstborn over all creation. For by Him all things were created that are in heaven and that are on earth, visible and invisible, whether thrones or dominions or principalities or powers. All things were created through Him and for Him. And He is before all things, and in Him all things consist. And He is the head of the body, the church, who is the beginning, the firstborn from the dead, that in all things He may have the preeminence.[9]

"God the Father qualified you," Paul was telling the church at Colosse, "to share in the inheritance that He has had in store for all His holy ones from before time. And that inheritance is Christ, in all of His inexhaustible riches. You, Colossians, are His holy ones—chosen, holy, and beloved of God." The same is true of you today. The Father pierced the kingdom of darkness; found you;

picked you up; and through the womb of death, carried you out of that dark kingdom. You then woke up in the glorious kingdom of light, the new Canaan, the realm of a sinless Son who is much loved by the Father.

Consider this much-loved Son. Set your eyes beyond the stratosphere and see a Christ who confounds the mind. This Christ *is*—present tense—the visible image of the invisible God. Jesus Christ displays God's image visibly in the invisible realm, where He is seated in heavenly places at the Father's right hand. To look upon the carpenter[10] of Nazareth is to discover God in totality. To know the suffering Nazarene is to know the Almighty, the one true Creator—He who was, is, and is to come.

But that's not all.

This Christ is the firstborn of the entire cosmos, the first person to appear in creation, and He is preeminent in all of it. All things visible and invisible were created by Him, through Him, to Him, and for Him. He is the Originator as well as the Goal—the Creator as well as the Consummator.

But that's still not all.

This Christ existed before time as the eternal Son. He is above time and outside of time. He is the beginning. In fact, He was before the beginning. He lives in a realm where there are no ticking watches and clocks. Space and time are but His servants. He is unfettered by them.

This Christ is not only before all things, but the entire universe is held together in Him. He is the cohesive force, the glue and gravitational pull that holds all created elements together. He is creation's great adhesive, the hinge upon which the whole cosmos turns. Remove Christ, and the entire universe disintegrates.

It comes apart at the seams. Remove Him, and creation's wheels come off.

But there's still more.

This Christ is the very meaning of creation. Eliminate Him, and the universe has no purpose. Remove Him, and every living thing loses its meaning.

But more than all of this, the One who created the universe watched it fall. He saw the cosmic revolt in heaven and the wreckage on earth. Under the caring eye of the Father, the Lord looked upon His own creation as it morphed into an enemy—His own enemy. And then He did the unthinkable: *He penetrated a fallen world.*

This Christ pierced the veil of space-time. He became incarnate and took on human flesh. As such, He was touched with the same temptations, the same infirmities, and the same weaknesses as all mortals, only He never yielded. Christ entered into His own creation to reconcile it back to Himself and to His Father. The Creator became the creature to make peace with an alienated creation.

But how?

By a wooden stake on a hill near Jerusalem, where blood was spilled. This Christ, the Jewish craftsman from Nazareth, was slaughtered outside the city gates. And by that horrible death, He reconciled a fallen cosmos to God.

The incarnate Son became the incarnation of sin and corruption. Every vile, foul, evil, dark, hideous vestige of the fall was laid upon His sinless body like a monstrous mantle of wickedness. The spotless one "became sin" incarnate.

But by His death, He slew all negative things. He brought the old creation to a complete end. Better, the old creation died having made peace with its Creator. And then, by His resurrection, He brought forth from the womb of death an unprecedented creation—of which you are a part.

So where there was hostility, He brought peace. Where there was separation, He brought union. Where there was death, He brought life.

But here's the mindblower: because of that hill, because of that blood, and because of that cross, you stand holy, spotless, blameless, without reproach and accusation in the sight of a holy God.

Yet that's not all.

This Christ created a new humanity, a new creation, a new race like Himself. That new humanity is His own body, a multi-membered creature we call the church, the *ekklesia* of God. It is bone of His bone and flesh of His flesh—kin to divinity. And this Christ is the head, the authority, and the source of that body.

But wait. There is more.

This Christ triumphed over the greatest enemy that God ever faced—*death*, the offspring of sin. He conquered its power, extinguished its sting, and dismantled the fear that was attached to it.

Jesus Christ passed through death and came out in resurrection—and He is the first to return from the dead to never taste mortality again.

But that's not all.

In His resurrection, this Christ—the only begotten Son—shook off His chains, no longer bound by time and space. He became a "life-giving Spirit," the firstborn among many sisters and brothers—all of whom will be raised from the dead after Him.

This glorious Christ defeated death, the grave, the curse, the entire world system; He defeated sin, satan, and all condemnation; He slew shame, He conquered guilt, and He shared His everlasting victory and towering triumph with you.

Here is a Christ so grand and glorious that He is beyond the reaches of human comprehension.

All things are in this Christ. All things are through this Christ. All things are for this Christ.

And He has been given the first place in everything.

What an incredible Lord!

This is how Paul described Him to the ailing Colossian church. The Jesus he presented makes one's brain cells smoke in the effort to grasp Him. He embodies the inexplicables of almighty God. And this is the same Jesus you have today.

MANIFESTING THE MYSTERY

After bringing the Colossian Christians into a view of the universe that would spin the head of Stephen Hawking and dumbfound Albert Einstein, Paul showed them the Father.

At some point, presumably before Creation, we can see the Father saying, "I have discovered My greatest pleasure. My greatest pleasure is that all of Me—all of My glory, all of My riches, all of My graces, all of My power—the totality of who I am as God, should dwell in My Son."

And so all the fullness of the Godhead—eternal Deity—poured into the Son of God to make its habitat in Him. (We discuss the triune nature of God more fully in chapter 10.)

In the midst of Paul's superlative descriptions of the craftsman from Nazareth, the apostle disclosed a mystery—"the mystery of the ages"—that had been shrouded and hidden in the very being of God for ages upon ages. All that Paul had said about Jesus in Colossians 1 led straight to this grand and glorious mystery, which was the main point of his letter.

And what was this mystery that had been hidden in God from before time?

It was not something to be solved or analyzed. It was not a principle, a rule, or a law. It was not even a set of answers to a set of questions, or a set of questions to spend one's life answering.

It was—and is—the wonder of all wonders.

The mystery of God is this . . .

that the One who is the visible image of the invisible God;
the One in whom all the fullness of the Godhead dwells;
the One who is the living residence of the Trinity;
the One in whom eternity lives, breathes, and has its being;
the One who is before time;
the A to Z, Alpha and Omega, the beginning and the end;
the Firstborn of the created universe, who rose from the dead never to die again;
the Conqueror of death, sin, and the grave;
the Creator, Savior, Redeemer, and Forgiver;
the One who holds all creation together in Himself;
the One who is the power of glory and might;

the Head, authority, and source of the
church;
the One through whom and for whom all
things were created;
the One in whom all things find their meaning
and reality;
the One who reconciled all things in heaven and
earth to God;
the One who nailed to His bloody cross every law,
every rule, and every regulation that would
condemn the beloved people of God;
the One who is supreme in every realm and holds the
first place in all things—the Son of the Father's love;
the One whose significance is unmatched in human
history;
the One who holds the title deed to the universe . . .

this glorious, limitless, amazing, incredible, expansive, incomparable, marvelous, stunning, staggering, majestic, mighty, matchless,
spectacular, outstanding, tremendous, immense, infinite, vast,
grand, triumphant, victorious, precious, radiant, peerless, wonderful, magnificent Christ has chosen to place all of His fullness
where?

Inside of you!

To [you] God willed to make known what are the riches of the
glory of this mystery among the Gentiles: which is Christ in
you, the hope of glory.[11]

As the Father was pleased to dwell in the Son, so Jesus Christ is pleased to dwell in you. All the riches of the glory of the heavens have been placed inside of you. *That* is the mystery of the ages—that this immense Lord, the living Word of God—has chosen to make His home within your being.

"Mindblowing" doesn't quite describe it, does it?

But there's even more.

Not only does this Christ live in you, but *more importantly: you* can live by His life.

> ...Christ who is *our life*.[12]

You have been invited to share *life* with your Maker and Creator.

And to top it all off, you have been made utterly, totally, fully complete in Him—here and now.[13]

Why, then, would you chase anything else? How can you be consumed with anything other than your Lord, Jesus Christ? And how can you graduate beyond Him?

He is enough, even more than enough.

Jesus Christ is like a vast ocean. He is too immense to fully explore, and too rich to fathom. You are like a bottle.

The wonder of the gospel is that the bottle is in the ocean, and the ocean is in the bottle.

This is the word of God that Paul of Tarsus, a "steward of the mystery," was called to preach and declare. This is the high gospel that was unveiled to a small group of ex-heathen Gentiles in the obscure town of Colosse in the first century. And this is the message that all who preach God's Word are called to proclaim today.

THE ALL-SUFFICIENCY OF CHRIST

Perhaps you've heard that phrase—"the all-sufficiency of Christ"—so many times that your mind is telling you to check out as we take another commercial break. Please don't do it. For what seems like a "commercial" is really the whole shebang.

The theme of Colossians is the fullness of Christ as the sufficiency of women and men. This theme is brought out in living color in chapter 2, where Paul began to apply the spellbinding revelation of Jesus from chapter 1 to the specific problems that the Colossians were facing.

According to Paul, a grand sighting of Christ will encourage your heart, knit it together with other believers, and bring you into all the wealth of wisdom and knowledge—which is Christ Himself.[14] He then went on to say, "Therefore as you have received Christ Jesus the Lord, so walk in Him, having been firmly rooted and now being built up in Him and established in your faith."[15] These words are a reference to the land of Canaan.

The land of Canaan is the greatest single picture of Christ in all the Old Testament. Everything that Israel needed to live, move, and have its being was contained there. Israel simply had to work the land, mine its riches, and live off of it.

Paul exhorted the Colossians Christians to "walk" in Christ and to be "rooted" and "built" in Him. So in effect, he was saying, "Walk in the *real* Canaan, which is Christ. Be built together with other living stones on His soil alone.[16] Make Him your life, your walk, your everything, and you will bear fruit."

In Old Testament times, the building of God—the temple—sat on the land of Canaan. It was built upon its very soil.

So Paul's message to the Colossians is clear: Sink your roots deep into Christ. If you build anything, build it on the land and take the building materials from the land. In other words, build it on Christ, with Christ, and for Christ.

Next, Paul got into the practical implications of walking in Christ. Allow us to paraphrase his message to the Colossians, because it's also a message to every believer today:

> You who would seek knowledge, lay hold of Him who is knowledge itself, the true *gnosis*.
>
> You who would chase after wisdom, seek Him who is the embodiment of all wisdom. All its treasures are found in Him.
>
> You who would chase after truth, come to Him who *is* the truth. In Him all truth dwells.
>
> You who would seek strength and power, find Him who is the very power and strength of God.
>
> You who wish to bear fruit, walk in love, and please the Lord, lay hold of Jesus Christ, who is the Vine, Love incarnate, and the only One in whom the Father is well pleased.[17]

Finally, Paul warned the Colossians of various challenges to their newfound faith that could arise and confuse them if they didn't know the answers. Here's how he advised them to respond, in so many words . . .

> If someone talks to you about circumcision, tell him that Christ is your circumcision, and you were circumcised in Him when you were baptized.
>
> If someone tries to sway you with persuasive words of human philosophy and traditions of men, turn a deaf ear.

Their origins are from this world, and they are a distraction from Christ.

If someone tells you to keep the Sabbath, to observe holy days and new moons, tell him that Christ is your Sabbath rest, your holy day, and your new moon.[18] These were but shadows. Jesus Christ is the reality, and you are complete in Him.

If someone says that you need a mystical vision to possess the fullness of God, tell her that Christ is your vision, and all of His fullness dwells in you.

If someone says that you must pursue angelic visitations, tell him that Christ is greater than any created being, including the angelic hosts. He is the head, the Lord, and the authority over every principality and power.[19] All rulers in the heavenly realms (angels, archangels, cherubim, seraphim, demons, and Lucifer himself) and on earth (kings, princes, presidents, and CEOs) are under the sovereign reign of Jesus Christ. They are but His servants.

If someone tells you that Christ dwells only in the institutional church, not in individual members of that body, tell her there is no such thing as an "individual member" of the body of Christ,[20] and that the "word of Christ"[21] rules both the full body and its personal members. You can even tell that individual that Jesus has a "live-in" relationship with you,[22] a living, dynamic presence in your personal life that is manifested in all you do, from worship to work, "in the name of the Lord Jesus."[23]

If someone tries to put you under the law, tell him that your Lord crucified the law, and He also crucified you, who couldn't keep it. He canceled the written code of laws that stood against you, and He nailed every broken commandment to His cross.[24]

But that's not all. Jesus Christ disarmed every dark power and unseen evil and made a public spectacle of them all, triumphing over them in His cross. Then He re-created you in His image, and His very presence in you has replaced the old written code. The law has died and has been raised again as a living person, Jesus Christ, who has come to live in you by His Spirit.

If someone says that in order for you to be holy, you must abuse your physical body and not touch, taste, or handle certain things, tell him that Jesus Christ is your holiness, your purity, and your righteousness.

In a word, hold fast to the head, and He will take care of everything else.

WHAT ABOUT OTHER THINGS?

Now, you may be thinking, *Okay, the message of the Bible is Christ; I got it. But we have to talk about other things too. Didn't Paul talk about singing, home life, master-slave relationships, and his coworkers in Colossians 3 and 4?*

Yes, he did. However, he addressed all of these topics in the light of Christ. These other subjects were like spokes in a wheel, the wheel being Christ Himself.

Notice how Paul naturally brought the Lord into all of these practical subjects:

Let the word of Christ dwell in you richly in all wisdom, teaching and admonishing one another in psalms and hymns and spiritual songs, singing with grace in your hearts to the Lord. And whatever you do in word or deed, do all in the name of the Lord Jesus, giving thanks to God the Father through Him.[25]

Wives, submit to your own husbands, as is fitting in the Lord.[26]

Masters, give your bondservants what is just and fair, knowing that you also have a Master in heaven.[27]

Tychicus, a beloved brother, faithful minister, and fellow servant in the Lord, will tell you all the news about me.[28]

Say to Archippus, "Take heed to the ministry which you have received in the Lord, that you may fulfill it."[29]

So Christ is found in the big picture, but He's also found in the smallest details. He's at the forefront of all spiritual things, yet He's present in the practical things as well.

How did Paul put it in Colossians 3:11? "Christ is all and in all."

In a church that is filled with leader-oholics, justice-oholics, commandment-oholics, and doctrine-oholics, it is essential that we comprehend how Paul (the go-to guy for all matters "doctrinal") understood his calling as an apostle. For Paul, his apostolate was not to advance a defining array of doctrines or a checklist of propositions. As far as he was concerned, our faith is not even a relationship with a set of doctrines or commandments.

Christianity is a relationship with Jesus the Christ. When things go wrong, it's not because we don't understand certain doctrines or fail to follow particular commands. It's because we have lost our "first love" . . . or never had it in the first place. We aren't in a "Vine and Wine" relationship with Jesus. Paul understood that, and that's why his gospel, his message, his "doctrine" was Christ. And he warned that no other doctrine be taught: "As I urged you when I went into Macedonia—remain in Ephesus that you may charge some that they teach no other doctrine."[30]

THE SIGHT OF PEERLESS WORTH

And their eyes were opened and they knew Him.[31]

We wish that every preacher, teacher, and leader would come to the realization that God's people—not to mention this world—need above all else a glorious unveiling of Jesus. But in the meantime, our hope is that God will "open the eyes of *your* heart" so that you may behold the incredible Christ. Once you understand "the glory of the riches of the mystery," you will find that the Jesus of the New Testament—the real Christ—is someone worth knowing intimately. All the treasures that are in Him are inexhaustible.

> To me, who am less than the least of all saints, this grace was given, that I should preach among the Gentiles the unsearchable riches of Christ.[32]

Never forget: There is much more in Christ than we have ever imagined. And there is infinitely more to Him that we have yet to know or touch. We can never exhaust Him. Christ is so large that no search party in the universe can explore an iota of His infinite depths. What is more, He will never grow old or stale. Jesus Christ is the only thing in God's universe that doesn't wear thin.

Yet so many Christians are blissfully unaware of His vastness. They have settled for so much less and have known Him so little.

But mark this down: When the people of God get a sighting of their incomparable Lord—and when the world encounters His unfathomable love, irresistible beauty, and overwhelming glory—every idol will be forced to the ground. The clouds of doubt will part from our eyes, and Jesus Christ will displace everything. But first, the church and the world must see Christ.

Therein lies the task of every disciple—to proclaim this amazing Christ to both lost and found.

Do you know your Lord as we have presented Him? Can you proclaim Him as Paul did in Colossians? Can you set God's people on fire with the same magnificent unveiling of Jesus?

If not, you will always be tempted to motivate God's people with lower things: principles, rules, regulations, religious duty, shame, fear, and guilt. You will continue to preach "things" instead of *Him*.

But we have not so learned Jesus Christ.

The greatest work of Jesus' friends (remember His words in John 15, "I no longer call you servants; I call you friends"?) is to cultivate an appetite, a hunger, in God's people for the Lord Jesus. The world awaits those who can present such a rich gospel that it leaves people spellbound, filled with awe, and desperate to know their inimitable Lord.

To close this chapter, we thought the words of a timeless hymn were fitting:

> *Hast thou heard Him, seen Him, known Him?*
> *Is not thine a captured heart?*
> *Chief among ten thousand own Him,*
> *Joyful choose the better part.*

Idols once they won thee, charmed thee,
Lovely things of time and sense;
Gilded thus does sin disarm thee,
Honeyed lest thou turn thee thence.

What has stript the seeming beauty
From the idols of the earth?
Not a sense of right or duty,
But the sight of peerless worth.

Not the crushing of those idols,
With its bitter void and smart;
But the beaming of His beauty,
The unveiling of His heart.

Who extinguishes their taper
Till he hails the rising sun?
Who discards the garb of winter
Till the summer has begun?

'Tis the look that melted Peter,
'Tis the face that Stephen saw,
'Tis the heart that wept with Mary,
Can alone from idols draw;

Draw and win and fill completely,
Till the cup o'erflow the brim;
What have we to do with idols
Who have companied with Him?[33]

CHAPTER 3

IF GOD WROTE YOUR BIOGRAPHY

We open this chapter by making an incredible statement: *If God were to write your biography, it would be Jesus Christ.*

Before you are tempted to throw this book through a window, bear with us a bit and read on.

The Christian life properly conceived and experienced is simply a reproduction and a reliving of the life of Jesus. Your Christian life begins with Christ, continues with Christ, and ends with Christ. Simply put, the history of Jesus is both the experience and the destiny of every believer.[1]

In other words, if God were to write your biography, it would be a fifth Gospel, so to speak. How did Paul put it? You are "living letters," or "epistle[s] of Christ . . . written not with ink but by the Spirit of the living God, not on tablets of stone but on tablets of flesh, that is, of the heart."[2]

On the heels of that statement, consider this question: *How would your biography read if God were to write it?*

Today, many Christians are inviting God into their stories. But God is inviting us into His. And that story is Jesus Christ. So, with a little sanctified imagination combined with the biblical text, the following is how your biography might read if God the Father were to write it. Note that it will read as if it were coming directly from the Father. We hope that as you read your story from God's perspective, you will hear your Father speaking to you in a personal way.

Your Real Birth

Your origins preceded your physical birth—just as the origins of My Son preceded His physical birth—and your beginnings reach back farther than antiquity.

You were chosen in My Son before the foundation of the world.[3] That's your starting point. Somewhere in the dateless past, before I said, "Let there be," I selected you—I "marked you out"—in My Son.[4] The origin of your existence, therefore, is found in Christ—the one who is "before all things."[5]

Your spiritual life in space-time finds its origins in Jesus also. When you received My Son, you were born a second time and from a different realm. You were "born from above."[6]

Don't be surprised when I say that you must be born from above.[7]

Birth is the impartation of life. When you were begotten again, an incorruptible seed of My life was placed into you by My Spirit. That seed was Christ. Within the DNA of that incorruptible seed is the nature and character of My Son. I have told you this several times in My Word:

> *[You have been] born again, not of corruptible seed but incorruptible, through the word of God which lives and abides forever.*[8]

> *Everyone who believes that Jesus is the Christ has been born of God, and everyone who loves the parent loves the child.*[9]

The life that you received at your new birth is known as "eternal life" and "everlasting life." Eternal life does not only point to longevity. It also points to the *kind* of life I have offered. It is, in fact, divine life—My own, uncreated life.

In other words, eternal life is My Son.

> *Jesus said . . . "I am the resurrection and the life."*[10]

> *And we know that the Son of God has come and has given us an understanding, that we may know Him who is true; and we are in Him who is true, in His Son Jesus Christ. This is the true God and eternal life.*[11]

When you were born anew, My Son was dispensed into you, and you became a partaker of My very nature.

> *His divine power has given to us all things that pertain to life and godliness . . . that through these you may be partakers of the divine nature.*[12]

But that's not all.

Your physical birth furnished you with a set of physical senses. In the same way, your new birth in Christ has furnished you with a set of senses. These are spiritual senses, the counterpart of your physical senses. The first of these is *spiritual sight.* It allows you to "see" with spiritual eyes.

We do not look at the things which are seen, but at the things which are not seen. For the things which are seen are temporary, but the things which are not seen are eternal.[13]

But we see Jesus . . .[14]

Your new birth also furnished you with spiritual hearing.

Behold, I stand at the door and knock. If anyone hears My voice and opens the door, I will come in to him and dine with him, and he with Me.[15]

He who has an ear, let him hear what the Spirit says to the churches.[16]

With your new birth also came the sense of spiritual taste.

[You] have tasted the heavenly gift, and have become partakers of the Holy Spirit.[17]

You have tasted that the Lord is gracious.[18]

Your new birth furnished you with new senses of spiritual touch and smell.

. . . holding fast to the Head.[19]

Now thanks be to God who always leads us in triumph in Christ, and through us diffuses the fragrance of His knowledge in every place.[20]

Once you were in darkness, and you could not see. You were lost, and your spiritual senses were dead.[21] But I brought you to life and carried you into the light, where you could see. Your spiritual senses were awakened, and you became part of a new creation in My Son.[22]

New birth also means you were given a new consciousness. You are now conscious of another realm outside the physical one wherein you stand. You are also conscious of another life within you. That life contains a new nature, new desires, new interests, new instincts, new inclinations, new tendencies, a new intelligence, and a new motivation. *That life is Christ Himself.*

So what you see, hear, taste, touch, and smell with your new senses is My Son. He is the object of your spiritual senses. And it is through those senses that you come to know Me, who is Spirit and not flesh.

Your Growth and Development

Spiritual growth and development mean having My Son formed in you.

My little children, . . . I labor in birth again until Christ is
formed in you[23]

Thus your growth as a disciple also comes back to Jesus. My goal is to have My Son wrought into your character so that He will be your all in all. To develop spiritually, then, is to *learn* My Son.

But you have not so learned Christ.[24]

But, speaking the truth in love . . . grow up in all things into
Him who is the head—Christ.[25]

Your growth as a Christian is growth in My Son, that is, development of that spiritual seed that I planted in you at your new birth. Growth in the Spirit takes place when more of your old nature dies and Christ gains more ground to live out His life in you. The stages of your spiritual life in My Son correspond to the stages of your physical life. You pass from babyhood,[26] to childhood,[27] to sonship—which is full spiritual stature.[28]

As you develop your spiritual senses, you are weaned from milk to meat. Yet "meat" is not just a tougher, more complex set of doctrines on which to masticate and ruminate. Meat is a greater apprehension and revelation of My Son, who embodies all truth and righteousness.[29] To put a finer point on it, spiritual growth is repeating the journey of Jesus while He was on earth. My Son is the inclusive human, the Last Adam. Whatever happened to Him happens to every one of My children. This is because I put you in My Son.

But of Him you are in Christ Jesus.[30]

As a result, you share in My Son's incarnation. While you do not share in His deity, you partake of His divine nature.[31] Because of this indwelling nature, you can confidently say, "*I can't, but Christ can.*" As you allow Him to live out His divine life through you, I am being expressed in your humanity. By this, you are a participant in the incarnation of Jesus, and you will begin to think like Him.

But we have the mind of Christ.[32]

When My Son was crucified, you were in Him, so you also died with Him. The person you used to be in fallen Adam was annihilated. Your flesh, your old nature, your *self*-nature, was done away with by the cross of Christ. In My records, you are already dead, because you died with My Son. Furthermore, all of your sins died with you. They no longer exist, according to My bookkeeping. And I'm the only one whose calculations count.

I have been crucified with Christ.[33]

Our old self was crucified with Him.[34]

Therefore . . . you died with Christ . . . [35]

In addition, when you voluntarily lose, lay down your life, die to yourself, and mortify the deeds of your flesh on a daily basis, you are further participating in your co-crucifixion with My Son.

*. . . that I may know Him and the power of His resurrection,
and the fellowship of His sufferings, being conformed to His
death.*[36]

Your joint death with Christ was the gateway to life.[37]
Everything new comes out of death—seeds, flowers, etc. The
natural is a picture of the spiritual. So in dying with Him, you
were on the road to new life.

But first, the dead had to be buried, and when My Son was
buried, you were in Him then too. Therefore, you were buried
with Him.

*Therefore we were buried with Him through baptism into
death*[38] *. . . buried with Him in baptism.*[39]

Your baptism in water reenacted your burial with My Son.
As you live your life free from the entanglements and entrap-
ments of the world system, you are daily participating in your
burial with Christ.[40] But you were not destined to stay buried.

When I raised My Son from the dead, I also raised you
from the dead, for you were in Him, and He in you.

You were raised with Him through faith in the working of
God, who raised Him from the dead.[41] If then you were raised
with Christ, seek those things which are above, where Christ is,
sitting at the right hand of God.[42]

Every time you allow the indwelling presence of My Son to
triumph over the forces of sin and death, you are living out the
dying and rising of Jesus in your mortal body.

When Christ ascended, you were in Him. Therefore, you

ascended with Him too, and are now seated in heavenly realms with Him.

> *[He] has raised us up together, and made us sit together in the heavenly places in Christ Jesus.*[43]

Whenever you enforce My Son's authority over My enemy by faith, you are participating in the ascendancy of Jesus, and you exercise all My authority over the powers of darkness.[44]

So concisely, the history of My Son, Jesus Christ, is *your* experience. Consequently, you are living both in the presence of the past (His incarnation, death, burial, resurrection, and ascension), and the future (His glorification and the fullness of His coming kingdom). There are only two things in His experience that you will not repeat. One is His being fully God. Although you are a partaker of the divine nature, you will never become divine. The other is His atoning work. You do not share in that. The work of atonement was uniquely His. But all of these other things have happened to and for you. Therefore, accept them as facts, take your place in My Son, and walk out your life from that high place. In Christ, there is no condemnation. Never forget that. You are *in* My Son, and you are a new creation.[45]

Your Glorious Destiny

This brings us to your final end—glorification. Glory is the highest expression of a life. The glory of a flower is reached when it is in full bloom. The glory of a human being is reached when women and men bear My image infinitely and at its full capacity.

I created humanity to share My glory—to exhibit My life in the highest possible way.

My Son lived, died, was buried, rose again, and ascended into the heavens to sit at My right hand, where He is now glorified. Because I placed you in Christ, you, too, have been glorified, even though you have not yet experienced it. It's already happened, however, for I see the end from the beginning and the beginning from the end and am in both places at the same moment. I hold time within My bosom.

> *Whom He predestined, these He also called; whom He called, these He also justified; and whom He justified, these He also glorified.*[46]

What's more, I wrapped it all up before I even began.

> *His work has been finished since the creation of the world.*[47]

I am the very meaning of the words "It is finished."[48] But now *you* have to finish what you've started. You can't start out as a baby and end as a baby. You must grow, mature, develop in My Spirit. Part of your spiritual development is service, which is simply allowing My Son to manifest His life through you as you serve others. The task of all ministry is to increase My Son, both in this world and in the church. It is to bring others into an increasing knowledge and apprehension of the significance of Christ. In other words, your goal in ministry should be to reveal the fullness of My Son. You do this by serving. It's one of the ways you grow into My Son's image.[49]

But know this: Your spiritual growth and development will

not occur as an individual. It will occur as a body. For My Son is not just Savior and Lord; He is the head of His body as well. The members of that body are connected. You will never grow into the fullness of My Son, therefore, as a separate, isolated individual, just as no part of your physical body can grow if it is detached from the other parts. The human body is a reflection of the body of Christ. Healthy spiritual growth occurs in the body as you are related to the other members. On your own, you will never reach the full measure of the stature of Christ. This is attained by the body as a whole.

In other words, it takes a church to raise a Christian.[50] And I designed it that way. Life in My Son has always been a corporate affair. My Word knows nothing of an independent, individualistic, insulated disciple.

For this reason, the master stroke of My enemy is division. If he can get you to divide from your sisters and brothers in Christ and be on your own—separate and isolated—you will not grow into the fullness of My Son.

So don't pull away from the body. Get connected to other believers who are pursuing My Son. Worship and serve as one part of the whole. You can only know My Son in His fullness in conjunction with the other members of His body, the church.

The End of All Things

What is the final object of your Christian life? What is the grand end and goal?

It is seeing the fullness of My Son. My object from beginning to end is Christ as all and in all. My desire is for My Son to fill the universe with His elegance.

He who descended is also the One who ascended far above
all the heavens, that He might fill all things[51] *... that in the*
dispensation of the fullness of the times He might gather
together in one all things in Christ, both which are in heaven
and which are on earth—in Him.[52]

If you are to reach My goal for you, you must steadily move toward the ultimate fullness that is in Him.

It is My good pleasure to fill the cosmos with My Son's glorious imprint and to sum up all things in Him. I created the universe by Him, through Him, to Him, and for Him. I was so in love with My Son that I wanted to share and increase Him. I wanted My creation to be full of His wonder and His radiance. Thus every time I painted the panorama of nature, I beheld My beloved Son. He was the template I used to craft the cosmos.

But creation fell from Me and became distorted, tarnished, and marred. My image was damaged in the earth. My glory was lost. Yet My Son willingly surrendered Himself to restore My passion. He came into My creation as a creature to redeem and reconcile a fallen universe to Himself. And He did it by a horrendous death, the crucifixion in which you were a part.

Since that time, the entire creation has been put back on course. It's now headed straight into My Son, where He shall fill all things with all of Himself. And that filling includes you.

For whom He foreknew, He also predestined to be conformed
to the image of His Son, that He might be the firstborn among
many brethren.[53]

*For it was fitting for Him, for whom are all things and by
whom are all things, in bringing many sons unto glory.*[54]

*When Christ who is our life appears, then you also will
appear with Him in glory.*[55]

But note that what will happen in the entire creation must
first be manifested in My people.

*Of His own will He brought us forth by the word of truth, that
we might be a kind of firstfruits of His creatures.*[56]

*For the earnest expectation of the creation eagerly waits for
the revealing of the sons of God.*[57]

My Son will bring His church—My people—into complete
conformity with His glorious person. When He was on earth,
My Son grew in stature.[58] Now, through Him, the church will
also grow in stature until that day when we, the body of Christ,
reach full maturity in glory.

*. . . till we all come to the unity of the faith and of the
knowledge of the Son of God, to a perfect man, to the
measure of the stature of the fullness of Christ.*[59]

The church will one day become the fullness of Christ and
the instrument through which He shall fill all things. In fact, I
have chosen the church to be the vessel through which My Son
will be revealed, fully presenced, and known.

Consequently, the *ekklesia* is the only hope this world has to see My Son physically before He returns. Why? Because His body is the living, breathing, moving, functioning image of Jesus. Therefore, the only address where anyone can find Him is . . . *you.*

> . . . *the church, which is His body, the fullness of Him who fills all in all.*[60]

My object and the object of My Spirit is to make My beloved Son everything, just as He made me everything. It is to give Him room so He can be displayed and expressed in all things—including your life. When He walked this earth, I dwelled in Him. When people saw Him in action, they were seeing Me in action. Now *He* dwells in you, and when people see you, they are seeing Him. And the more space you make for Him in your life, the more clearly the world will see Him.

So give Him room. Let Him gain all of you so He can be seen again, to My glory and pleasure. I created the visible universe so that eyes would behold the beauty of My Son and fall in love with Him. This is the mission to which you have been called.

THE AUTHOR AND FINISHER OF OUR FAITH

So that's how God might have written your biography.

As we said in the opening of this chapter, your biography begins, continues, and ends with Jesus Christ. He chose you before time, you were born into Him in due time, Christ is being formed in you in the present time, and you will be matured and perfected in Christ at a future time. In the words of Scripture, Jesus is "the author *and* finisher of our faith."[61]

With the exception of Christ's deity and atoning work, the spiritual biography of every child of God is a repetition of *His* life. As you yield to the Holy Spirit, He will take the history of Jesus and duplicate it in you.

It is Christ from beginning to end. He is the object of the Christian life, and the forerunner of our experience.

The forerunner has entered for us, even Jesus.[62]

So why do we preach and teach all sorts of other things?

As we write these words, there's a lot of talk about being "missional." But to be truly missional means constructing one's life and ministry on Christ. He is both the heart and bloodstream of God's plan. To miss this is to miss the plot. Indeed, it is to miss everything.

God's grand mission is what the New Testament calls "the eternal purpose."[63] And in the dead center of that purpose is the living Christ. Christ is God's dream, and His eternal purpose in Christ Jesus is vastly encompassing; it answers every particular. Nothing that God wants is omitted from it. The Father's

> Your mother is a cause of wonder: the Lord entered into her and became a servant; he who is the Word entered—and became silent within her; Thunder entered her and made no sounds; there entered The Shepherd of all, and in her He became the Lamb . . .
>
> —Ephrem the Syrian (Fourth century)[64]

timeless intention reaches from one end of Himself to another, forever. And the focus of His eternal purpose was, is, and always has been *Christ in you*—the divine secret hidden in the counsels of God from before time.[65]

If Christ is in you, then the Christian life is not about striving to be something you are not. It is about becoming what you *already* are.

For to me, to live is Christ.[66]

As He is, so are we in this world.[67]

You were once darkness, but now you are light in the Lord. Walk as children of light.[68]

> Christ Jesus . . . you inspired generations of pilgrims in the way of love and hope. Enfold your Church in the mystery of your life, that we, in our own pilgrimage, may be apostles of your wounded and risen glory.
> The Edmund Prayer[69]

So why do we preach rules, regulations, and laws instead of Christ? And why such an emphasis on "works"? Good works are simply fruit falling off a tree. If you will sink your roots deep in Christ, who is your life, you will not be able to stop the fruit from coming forth.

Heaven has chosen this Jesus to be before all, through all, in all, and to all, until He is all in all.

Everything else is postscript.

The engine of being "missional," therefore, ought never to be religious duty. Neither should it be guilt, condemnation, or ambition. The engine should be blindly and singularly a revelation of Jesus Christ.

No matter how long we live, how much ministry we engage in, how much Scripture we learn, how much theology we study, and how many hours we spend praying, we will never get beyond God's eternal purpose. Or to put it another way, it doesn't get any better than Christ.

But perhaps the most arresting fact of all is that this wonderful Christ is in love with you. And His love never fails, gives up, or disappears. The knowledge-surpassing love of Christ is perfect love, and He's committed to completing in you what He has started.

We love Him because He first loved us.[70]

He who has begun a good work in you will complete it until the day of Jesus Christ.[71]

When, in the Middle Ages, Jesus was referred to as "our kinde Lord," this did not mean just that He was gentle, but that we were bound to Christ by the bonds of kinship. His kindness is the love of a brother.

—Timothy Radcliffe[72]

True Christianity is the life that Jesus lived in the past, lived out in you in the present. And it is in Him that we find our true humanity. For this reason, it takes God to be a human.

To put it all in a sentence: *From the viewpoint of God, your biography is Jesus Christ.*

> Clearly you are an epistle of Christ, ministered by us, written not with ink but by the Spirit of the living God.[73]

CHAPTER 4

A VIOLIN CALLED MESSIAH

The Old Testament teaches us that if you seek God, you will find Him.[1] Jesus went one better: He said that God seeks *you.* Jesus Christ, God the Son, knocks at your door and asks if you can come out and play.[2]

> God is nearer to me than I am to myself.
>
> —Meister Eckhart[3]

God doesn't wait for us to come to Him. God comes to us in Jesus, making Himself at home with us. Jesus is the dramatic pitching of God's tent, wherein God is with us, making beautiful music for us to dance to—if we only will.[4]

PLAYING THE MESSIAH'S MUSIC

The name Stradivarius is synonymous with the most expensive, most famous, most desirable violins in the world—even if they are three-hundred-year-old instruments.

61

Antonio Stradivari set up his workshop in the small Italian town of Cremona in the 1600s. During this time the best violins in the world were being made by the Amati family. But the Amati violins were made for the drawing room or the court, and music-making was changing. It was moving from the drawing room to the concert hall, where it would have to be heard clearly in the back reaches of the room. Stradivari both reflected and reinforced this metamorphosis. He chose bigger and better pieces of maple, experimented with stronger varnishes, and arched the belly of the violin differently.[5] These changes gave Stradivari's violins a distinctive sound, unlike any before their time. (If Stradivari were alive today, he would no doubt trademark the sound of his violins, just as Harley-Davidson trademarked the "Hog Call," the rev of a Harley, which has become one of the most recognized sounds in the world today.)

> 'Tis God gives skill
> But not without men's
> hands: He could
> not make Antonio
> Stradivari's violins
> without Antonio. Get
> thee to thy easel.
> —George Eliot[6]

When Stradivari died in 1737, a particular violin was found in his studio. It had never been played. This violin, called "the Messiah," had an incredible tiger-striped pattern on its back. It was said to be the "perfect violin." Today the Messiah is in the Ashmolean Museum in Oxford, and it is the only known instrument to have its own showcase.[7]

But wait a minute. The "perfect violin" is one that has *never been played*? Not according to Ivry Gitlis, a violinist who plays his Stradivari every day. He says of his perfect violin, "I have a violin that was born in 1713. I don't consider it my violin. Rather, I am its violinist; I am passing through its life."[8]

Indeed, life is like the gift of a Messiah violin. We don't own the instrument. For a time, we get to play on it our original song and sounds, and in our own way. But our lives are not our own. We are in *the* Messiah's symphony, where each instrument, no matter how different, brings itself into accord with the Composer and the Conductor.

CALL IT LIKE YOU SEE IT

The beginning of wisdom, advises a Chinese proverb, is to call things by their right names. The "New" King James Version of the Bible was not an advance when it changed the 1611 language from "follow" to "imitate," as in "Imitate me, just as I also imitate Christ."[9] The American Standard Version is even worse. It changes the word from "follow" to "imitate" virtually everywhere.[10]

But being a follower of Jesus does not involve imitation as much as it does implantation and impartation. Failure to understand the difference between "imitation" and "implantation" reveals a failure to understand the nature of "incarnation."

Incarnation—the notion that God connects to us in baby form and human touch—is the most shocking doctrine of the Christian religion. It is the mystery of God's self-emptying in Jesus Christ so that we could one day be indwelt by the Holy Spirit.[11] Or, as Augustine put it in one of his most striking phrases, "The deformity of Christ forms in you." He explained, "If [Christ] had not been willing to be deformed, you would not have recovered the form you lost."[12] God, in the form of Jesus, became a human.

He was then deformed by becoming sin, so that by His deformation we might find re-formation into the image of God.

In the incarnation, the beating heart of the universe became a human heart.[13] God became a participant in the human spillage of resentment, vanity, selfishness, and death so that we might become participants in the divine nature of love and life. In other words, God the Divine became God in human skin—living, dying, and rising. He "emptied" Himself so that He could experience all that we would—and then be reborn again to eternal life so that we could too. But because Christ was willing to "empty" Himself, He expects the same of us—today. If we are to be reborn to everlasting life, then we must willingly empty *our*selves—of our wants, our dreams, and our agendas. We are not in control of our lives; *He* is. In fact, here is God's version of "self"-control, in a nutshell: "Christ in you, the hope of glory."[14]

"Breathe on Me, Breath of God" is more than a metaphor and a hymn. It's a testimony to the risen Christ who breathes in you and me. Christ dwells in us. Why don't we also let Him breathe through us by living our lives as an offering to Him? Singer/songwriter Maria McKee has a song called "Breathe" in which she does exactly that: she presents an offering of herself to Christ:

> *I will let you breathe through me*
> *I will let you be with me . . .*
> *My heart beats your blood;*
> *your breath fills my lungs.*[15]

But the doctrine of implantation/impartation has perhaps never been better expressed than in the words of Symeon the New

Theologian (949–1022), one of only three saints of the Orthodox church to have been granted the title "theologian":

> *We awaken in Christ's body*
> *as Christ awakens our bodies . . .*
> *and everything that is hurt, everything*
> *that seemed to us dark, harsh, shameful,*
> *maimed, ugly, irreparably*
> *damaged, is in him transformed,*
> *recognized as whole, as lovely,*
> *and radiant in his light.*"[16]

LIFE'S "GOTCHA" MOMENT

In faith, there is a "gotcha" moment, when Jesus gets you for life. The gotcha moment may take millions of minutes or just one. But when Jesus gets you for life, you begin to live out of Jesus-love. When we present ourselves as "living offerings" to Christ, suddenly questions of what to do and what not to do take on a whole new meaning. Once we are truly sharing our lives with Christ and learning to live in His love, then truly *Charitas Christi urget nos*: "The love of Christ constrains us."[17]

It is not the commandments and the laws that control our behavior. It is the presence of the indwelling Christ and Jesus-love that both restrains and releases us. A relational Christ ethic is why Paul said Christians don't have sex with prostitutes. Since Christ is living His resurrected life in and through you, would you want Jesus to share that purchase of lust with you?[18] Would Jesus treat any woman like a purchase? The commandments are paper handcuffs compared to Jesus' love strands. It is "the love of Christ" that impels, compels, and propels us—a love that is so captivating we become free to do it all . . . in love, with love, for love.

Of the millions of words dictated by the gifted Latin-speaking Christian Augustine, bishop of Hippo (354–430), these are perhaps the most important but also the most misread: *Dilige, et quod vis fac*, "Love God, and do what you will."[19] If you love God, or love another, the one thing you cannot do is what you will, for love bends the will. To live in God's love is not license for hedonism, but liberty for sacrificial living where we're all working off the same brief, which reads, "As I have loved you, so you must love one another"[20] and "Greater love has no one than this, that he lay down his life for his friends."[21]

> No one can know God who does not first know him/herself.
> —Meister Eckhart [22]

To live the "incarnate life" is to do little large. God does little large. That is the story of the incarnation, and that is the metanarrative of the Bible. At the heart of orthodoxy is paradoxy: the paradox of the littlest revealing the largest and the finite revealing the infinite. The incarnation is both once-and-for-all and ongoing, as the One who "was and who is to come"[23] now is, and lives His resurrection life in and through us. An "already now" participates in the "still not yet."

A DIVINE APERTURE

An "aperture" is an opening through which light travels. The narrower the hole, the more focused the image becomes. The wider the aperture, the less clearly defined the image you are trying to capture will be. You can have all the light in the night sky coming through a wide aperture and have very little usable image. You can have everything present in every space, but it will be entirely useless as a dependable, definable image.

Christ is the Aperture of God. In the small opening of this one life, the clearest image of the whole can be seen. In Christ, God the infinite became finite. All the rays of truth in the universe focus through him: "The Son is the radiance of God's glory and the exact representation of his being, sustaining all things by his powerful word."[24]

It all began with one person in one place . . . until the local was made the universal, the little made large, by the power of God's Spirit. At the height of the universal, when Jesus was dying on the cross to show God's love for the world, He attended to the particular. He showed His love for two of the people He loved most—His mother and His best friend.

THE TWO SIDES OF INCARNATION

There are two sides of incarnation. One is "God sent His Son" and thus "abased Himself." On the other side, God raised humanity and pulled us into something bigger than we are—a trinitarian vortex that we get to be part of.[25] Incarnation doesn't just apply to Jesus; it applies to every one of us. Of course, not in the same redemptive way. But close.

Whether in alliance or in defiance, the question of Mary is also our question: How can this be? How can Jesus be born in me and grow in me? How can the Messiah be bodily present with us today?

We have been given God's "Spirit," which makes Christ "real" in our lives. We can actually now, as Peter puts it, "participate in the divine nature."[26] How, then, in the face of so great a truth, can we ask for toys and trinkets? How can we lust after lesser gifts and itch for religious and spiritual "thingies"? We've been touched from on high by the fires of the Almighty and given divine life, a life that has passed through death—the very resurrection life of the Son of God Himself. How can we not be fired up?

> There were moments when Our Lord's divinity slipped from him into the world which he created.
>
> —Keble College Warden Austin Farrer[27]

IMITATION VS. IMPLANTATION

There is a vast ocean of difference between trying to compel Christians to imitate Jesus and learning how to impart an implanted Christ. The former only ends up in failure and frustration. The latter is the gateway to life and joy in our daying and our dying. We stand with Paul—"Christ lives in me"[28]—and we aspire with him to "have the mind of Christ."[29] Our life is Christ. In Him we live, breathe, and have our being.[30] "What would Jesus do?" is not Christianity. Christianity asks, "What is Christ doing *through me* . . . through *us*? And how is He doing it?" Following Jesus means to "trust and obey," as the old hymn goes. But faith and obedience to Christ isn't self-effort. It's responding to God's will and living by His indwelling life through the power of the Spirit.

Doing life together with Jesus is a coauthored narrative

process filled with many points of crisis. But the imaginative, tension-filled process of engaging the crisis is what makes a story interesting.

Every crisis raises relational issues: Will you try it and handle it yourself? Will you find a new partner? Or will you and Jesus tackle the crisis together? In tackling the stuff of life together, you'll see that your relationship with God will deepen.

In pondering Christ, you find that you are in fact living His life, and God is living yours. Christ in you and you in Christ. God doesn't lead you through phases or steps. He draws you to Himself in continuous motion. What we often have viewed as stages or phases may be a change in music. But the point is never the music. It is the dance. The music is often part of the dance. But sometimes the most beautiful dance is the one where you and your partner make up the music as you dance together.

A THEOLOGY OF LIKENESS

There is a pervasive theology of "likeness"—"O God, make me more Christlike"—that cheapens the gospel and depresses the spirit. Christlikeness is too small a dream, too shallow an ambition, for a Christian. The call to Christlikeness is also not "good news."

First of all, too much of the "like Jesus" talk smacks of an "as if" faith. Take Christian "nonrealist" Don Cupitt, who doesn't believe there are actual "entities" of God or Christ. Still, if we accept Jesus' stories "as if they are true," he argues, then we can "live like Christ."[31] But the stories and metaphors of Jesus, and of the faith, should elicit more in us than "I shall strive to live *as if* these things were true." Christian faith is more than having superior stories. To be His follower means more than admiring His courage and gleaning lessons from His teachings. In an "as if" faith, there is no difference between following Jesus and following ethical behavior. (More on this later.)

Second, we want a "like-Christ" relationship with God on our terms. But a loving, living relationship with Christ begins on God's terms. In other words, it begins with the cross, or more precisely, a "dying with Christ." It begins with a "death" to all those parts of us that are damping and hampering the Spirit's work and preventing us from being "liberated from the controlling powers of [the] world,"[32] the destructive, dehumanizing, controlling forces, like addictions, selfism, consumerism, hedonism, and others.

Third, to be "like Christ" often implies that you don't really need Christ, since you already have the ideas and teachings of Christ.

Here is a posted response on Facebook to our attempts at refocusing on Jesus:

> i really think it doesn't matter that much to god if we are christ-centered or not . . . in fact, i don't believe the gospel is about being christ-centered at all . . . jesus himself is not christ-centered . . . so why should we insist that the gospel is christ-centered . . . the son points all of God's creation to his father, the one and only true god . . . by putting the emphasis on even a "christ-centered way," we are making the being of jesus a narcissistic figure . . . true, he was a major actor because it is his life that is being played out . . . but lest we forget . . . the creator sen[t] us a redeemer to bring us back to the creator!!! i don't read any "christ-centered-ness" here nor do we need to

be cautioned that not everything is "christ-centered" . . . that's
because this term that evangelicals have constructed is not even
a biblically correct concept.

This comment misses the point on so many levels. One of
them is that what the Father was to Jesus, Jesus is now to us (see
chapter 8).

Fourth, as Martin Luther said, if you read the Law, you will
see that you can never hope to keep it. Similarly, try to be like
Christ, and you will quickly realize that you don't have a prayer
of becoming like Him. If you were a musician, and you were told
that the goal of your life was to be like Mozart, would this be good
news to you? If you were an artist, and you were told that your life
ambition was to be like Michelangelo, would you jump up and
down in excitement? Most of you could sit at a piano every wak-
ing moment, or stand at an easel for twelve hours a day, or sculpt
a stone without stopping except to eat and sleep, and you could
still never be like Michelangelo or Mozart.

So be "like" Christ? Hmm . . .

Always turn the other cheek?

Always walk the second mile?

Always love your enemies?

Never think an unsanctified thought?

Never have even a hint of a pity party?

Always be prepared to give a "word in season"?

Pay attention to the words "always" and "never."

The fact is, Jesus was the greatest human being who ever lived,
and if all we have to look forward to in life is the frustration of

trying to be someone we are not, then we've got better ways of enjoying the interval between birth and death.

But the "good news" is that Jesus *doesn't* want us to be "like" Him. He wants to share His resurrection life with us. He doesn't want us to imitate Him; instead, Christ, the Unspeakable Gift,[33] wants to live in and through us.

The gospel is not the imitation of Christ; it is the implantation and impartation of Christ. We are called to do more than mediate truth. We are called to manifest Jesus' presence.

That "we" means *you*.

Contrast the designations "Paul of Tarsus" with "Jesus of Nazareth." Tarsus was the capital city of Cilicia, a place proud of its Greek culture. The title "Paul of Tarsus" was like saying "Paul of London" or "Paul of New York City." There are at least twenty-five references to Jesus as "Jesus of Nazareth." This is our equivalent of saying, "Jesus of the slums" or "Jesus of the ghetto" or "Jesus of the *favelas*" or "Jesus of the squatter camps." Nazareth was the armpit of Galilee that stunk worse from the stench of nearby Samaritans. Every nation has a Nazareth. Every person has a Nazareth.

Where's your Nazareth? Where's that written-off place, that written-off person, that written-off part of your life? God can take a nobody person from a nowhere place and make "a Jesus of [fill in the blank]" out of him or her.

> *I've found a Friend; O such a Friend!*
> *He bled, He died to save me;*
> *And not alone the gift of life,*
> *But His own self He gave me.*
> *Naught that I have mine own I'll call,*

I'll hold it for the Giver;
My heart, my strength, my life, my all,
Are His, and His for ever.[34]

JESUS IS NO VENEER

Does anyone really like veneered furniture? Yes, it saves wood. Yes, it is cheaper. Yes, it is easier to work with. But Jesus is *not* a veneer that covers up inferior wood.[35] Jesus works all the way down and through until, as Paul put it, "I no longer live, but Christ lives in me."[36] It should be said of you, "In [insert your name], something of Christ lives. The Jesus story continues in his/her life."

A French pastor was called to serve in a small French community. At one of the first homes he visited, the wife was away, so he could only talk with the husband. When the wife returned, she probed her husband about the nature of the new pastor's visit:

"What did he say?" she asked.

"He asked, 'Does Christ live here?'" the husband replied. "He didn't really ask anything else. Just, 'Does Christ live here?'"

"Well, surely you told him that we are the church's biggest supporters."

"He didn't ask that," the husband repeated. "He only asked, 'Does Christ live here?'"

"Well, you must have told him that we read our Bible and say our prayers every day."

"He didn't ask about that either. He only asked, 'Does Christ live here?'"

"Well, did you tell him that we attend his services every Sunday and sit in the front?" the wife persisted.

"He *didn't ask about that.* He only wanted to know, 'Does Christ live here?'"

And that's all God wants to know.

Christ wants to be born in you and to live in and through you. It's as if you were that budding musician who was told, "Give your life to music, and Mozart will so come to life in you that when you sit down at the piano and play, it will not be you alone playing, but you and Mozart together." Or as if you were an aspiring artist who was promised, "Give your life to painting, and Michelangelo will so come to life in you that when you stand at that easel, it will be you *and* Michelangelo wielding the brush."

Cecilia Siqueria (Uruguay) and Fernando Lima (Brazil) met in the Brazilian town of Cruzeiro-do-Sul in July 2001, where the master guitarist and young prodigy shared the first prize at the International Acoustic Guitar Competition. Since then, they have sometimes appeared together, playing the same guitar.[37] Wouldn't it be awesome for Christ to be manifested with you, no matter what you're doing?

Ω

> Love is giving something one doesn't have to someone who doesn't want it."
> —Slovenian philosopher and sociologist Slavoj Žižek[39]

The good news is as scary as it is good. It is safe to be "like" Jesus; it is scary to "be" and "do" Jesus. Yet, wrote Archibald MacLeish, "A poem should not mean / but be."[38] Likewise, a Christian should not mean, but be. Be what? The living Christ for a dying world. But to "be" is to give up control and ownership and to share life with the Word made flesh,[40] the very image of the invisible God.[41] The truth is that if we all fully understood what it means that the very being of God wants to take residence in us and share our life, we would all be reluctant incarnations.

Yet, "Let it be," Mary said to the angel, never knowing what the "it" would be.

THE CULT OF CUTENESS

Disciples of Jesus, beware of cute. Christians are on high alert for cute. We love cuteness. This is a cute-driven culture. It turns everything it touches into glitz and attractiveness and gets rid of anything that isn't "cute."

But the story of Jesus' birth, death, and resurrection doesn't compute with cute:

- The Annunciation, when the angel Gabriel appeared to the virgin Mary to tell her she was pregnant, wasn't cute.
- Admitting to Joseph that she was pregnant wasn't cute.
- The Magnificat wasn't cute.[42]
- The little town of Bethlehem wasn't cute.
- The killing of the innocents wasn't cute.
- Jesus' genealogy is not cute. (His lineage includes a rape victim, an adulteress, and a prostitute.)
- The kiss in the garden wasn't cute.
- Golgotha wasn't cute.

The word *crux* in Latin means "cross." The crux of Christianity is the cross. And the cross certainly isn't cute. The old Christian calendar had ways of resisting this cultural drift into cuteness even at the "cute" moment of Jesus' birth.

Christ wants to be conceived anew in your heart, in your hopes, in your family, in your community—but not as a cutesy little baby who's still in the manger. Jesus Christ is the author and perfecter of our faith,[43] not a babe wrapped in swaddling clothing. So for Him to be conceived anew in *you*, you must enter into a faith-filled, dynamic, life-giving *relationship* with Him through the Spirit of God[44] so that He radiates from you in all you do.

But what kind of journey might the "Radiance of God's glory"[45] put you on? It could be a hard one; not all journeys are easy. When Mary affirmed, "Let it be with me according to Your word," she could not foresee all that the little word *it* would bring to her life. "It" was definitely not easy—or cute.

"It" would mean a pregnancy out of wedlock.

"It" would include giving birth far from her home.

"It" would be a death sentence on her child's life, and a night flight into Egypt.

"It" would be long years of a simple, ordinary life in a no-name village.

"It" would be three years of trying to understand the transformation of her son into the Son of God, and . . .

"It" would be the horror of the cross, and a mother's heartbreak at the tomb.

But "it" was worth it all when it became, finally, the glory of the resurrection. Then we beheld the glory of the bright Morning Star.[46]

There is always an "it" that brings faith out of "cuteness" and into acuteness of mission and ministry. But "it" is never what it appears to be with a "hope of glory"[47] who trades in promises and possibilities. When we can say with Paul, "In the cross of Christ I glory,"[48] we are claiming impossibility as the element in which we live and move and have our being.

BAD DAYS—BUT A BETTER VIOLIN

There is an old Chinese parable about an elderly man and his only son who live together in a small rural community. One night, the father's horse wanders off, and his neighbors come to express their sympathy for his loss. But the old man says to them, "How do you know this is ill fortune?"

A few days later, the horse returns, followed by an entire herd of wild horses. Now the neighbors come to congratulate the old man on his good luck. But the old man says, "How do you know this is good fortune?"

Time passes, during which the son takes to riding the wild horses—until one of them throws him, and he breaks a leg. Again the neighbors come, this time to express sorrow for the old man's bad luck. "How do you know it is bad luck?" asks the old man.

A short time later, a Chinese warlord comes into the town to recruit all able-bodied young men for his next little war, but the son escapes the draft because of his broken leg. This time the neighbors tell the old man how pleased they are at his good fortune. And one more time the old man replies, "How do you know this is good fortune?"

And here the story ends—although it could, of course, go on and on.

ΑΩ

There is mystery to life. Sure, it seemed like a bad day when the old man lost his horse. And sure, it seems like a bad day when some tragic moment intrudes into our lives. But the Christian withholds final judgment of whether it's a "good day" or a "bad day" until all the days are in.

It seemed like a bad day when Jesus hung on a cross. But that "bad day" was quickly followed by a good day—the one that we still live in now: the day when a certain violin began to play its tune through a resurrected human.

CHAPTER 5

A DITCH ON EITHER SIDE

The great theologian Karl Barth once wrote that truth walks the razor edge of heresy.[1] Indeed, the road to truth is surrounded by a ditch on either side.

> Be careful to do as the LORD your God has commanded you; you shall not turn aside to the right hand or to the left.[2]

With this thought in mind, let's look at two popular approaches to following Jesus among Christians today. They are: (1) theological rationalism and (2) theological ethics.

Theological rationalism: This approach holds that Christianity is the life application of the correct description of God, found in the right doctrinal system. Those who hold to this idea reason that the correct belief system is at the heart of authentic Christianity. God, Jesus, the Holy Spirit, and the world are only truly understood within the bounds of such a system.

Theological ethics: This approach holds that the center of Christianity is a rule of ethical behavior (sometimes equated with "the kingdom of God"). Its supporters maintain that Christians are not adherents to a system of thought. They are instead followers of the greatest moral teacher of all time—Jesus of Nazareth. Theological rationalism, they believe, leads to an intolerant and aggressive pushing of one's opinion. By contrast, Jesus is simply the carrier of what's really important: the right *ethical* approach to life. We are called to follow not the living Christ but a set of moral principles that are attributed to Him.

The Bible is critical of both approaches. Each represents a ditch on either side of the razor edge of truth.

CHRISTIANITY IS NOT WHAT YOU THINK

According to Scripture, Jesus Christ (and not a doctrine about Him) is the truth. In addition, Jesus Christ (and not an ethic derived from His teaching) is the way. In other words, both God's *truth* and God's *way* are embodied in a living, breathing person—Christ.

"I am the way, the truth, and the life."[3]

There is a billboard in Oklahoma that reads, "Eternity is hell without Jesus." But in truth, every place and any place is hell without Jesus. Hawaii is hell without Jesus. The Ritz Carlton is hell without Jesus. And a "church" is hell without Jesus. There is no hope in this life or in this world apart from Christ.

This seems like a strange claim in a world centered on either epistemological proofs of what constitutes true knowledge (as in the works of Descartes, Locke, and Hume and their intellectual off-spring) or in a concept of ethics that is meant to guide humans individu-ally and collectively (as in the writings of Kant and Bentham). John Rawls has recently tried to combine both traditions into a "theory of justice" by yoking the structure of Hume with the spirit of Kant.[5]

> There is a great difference between a mystery of God that no one understands, and a mystery of God laid hold of, let it be but by one single man.
> —George MacDonald[4]

But the Lord Jesus Christ Himself—and not a theory of "the true" or "the good"—is at the heart of Christianity.

When Christ is understood in terms of a cohesive theological system, Jesus becomes subordinated to a human description. The "idea" of Jesus is treated as the equivalent of the *reality* of Christ. We are then hindered from growing in His life, being tied down to a frozen construction of Him. We also become insulated from the challenges posed by the reality of Jesus, which always exceeds our present descriptions of Him.

When Christ is understood in terms of an ethical standard, He becomes simply a means. There is one thing that all ethical teachers have in common. In every case, they are only a means to an end. They are merely the vehicles of something far more important—their ethical teaching. Once a person has learned the teaching, he or she could lose the memory and identity of the teacher and still possess his teaching.

But as Sören Kierkegaard and others pointed out, this is not the case with Christianity. Jesus Christ is the main event. He, not the ethical teachings He delivered, is the end and goal. (The Sermon on the Mount is frequently manhandled this way.)

When Paul exhorted us to put on the "mind" of Christ,[6] the Greek word he used for "mind" had nothing to do with cognitive skill or intellectual brainpower. To have the mind of Christ does not mean possessing the *knowledge* of Christ or the intellectual comprehension of Christ but the relational *knowing* of Christ.

Jesus cannot be separated from His teachings. Aristotle said to his disciples, "Follow *my teachings.*" Socrates likewise said to his disciples, "Follow *my teachings.*" Buddha said to his disciples, "Follow *my meditations.*" Confucius said to his disciples, "Follow *my sayings.*" And Muhammad said to his disciples, "Follow my *noble pillars.*"

But Jesus says to His disciples, "Follow *Me.*"

In all the religions and philosophies of the world, a follower can follow the teachings of its founder without having a relationship with that founder. But not so with Jesus Christ. The teachings of Jesus cannot be separated from Jesus Himself. Christ is still alive, and He embodies His teachings. This is what separates Him from every great teacher and moral philosopher in history.

This is not to say that other religious traditions don't focus on a person. Buddhism can't be imagined without Buddha. Islam can't be imagined without Muhammad: "Muhammad is his [Allah's] Messenger," say the Muslim people. Judaism doesn't so much focus on a person as on a nation—the Jewish people as a whole, and the religion they follow.[7]

Yet in all these religions, a follower can abide by all the teachings of its founder without having a *relationship* with that founder. Not so with Jesus Christ.

Perhaps the most respected U.S. scholar of Judaism in the twentieth century, Jacob Neusner, wrote a book in which he projected himself back into the gospel of Matthew to query Jesus on the Jewish law. Neusner's studied conclusion is that Jesus really didn't understand the Torah. Why? Because He left something out? No, Neusner contends that it was because He put something in that wasn't there: *Himself*.[8] Neusner argues that since Jesus inserted Himself above the Torah, any thoughtful Jew must reject Jesus because He was "abandoning the Torah" at worst or demoting the Torah at best, by claiming so much for Himself.

Only about 0.5 percent of all Jews alive during Jesus' ministry were aware of Him.[9] Almost all who knew Jesus rejected Him as the Messiah because He didn't come up with the real messianic goods. According to Ezekiel, this included: (1) the ingathering of exiles; (2) the reign of the messianic king; (3) scrupulous observance of the commandments; (4) a new Temple; (5) peace; and (6) universal worship of the one true God.[10]

Instead of the idiom of law and commandments, Jesus taught an idiom of love and relationships. Jesus is the Love of God, which is another way of saying He is the *Son* of God. Jesus was an evangelist of the God who is love; He was an evangelist not of principles and beliefs and leadership skills, but of a reign of divine love. Thus, Christianity is highly relational and highly communitarian. It's neither individualistic nor abstract. Christianity centers not on points, principles, and propositions, but on a person and a people.[11]

It is a profound mistake, therefore, to treat Jesus as simply the founder of a set of moral, ethical, or social teachings. The Lord Jesus and His teaching are one. The Medium and the Message are one. Christ is the incarnation of the kingdom of God and the Sermon on the Mount. He is the sum and the substance of His teachings. Therefore, Christianity has nothing to do with our vaunted religious subjectivity, and everything to do with the greatness of God's gift of Himself in the first-century Jewish rabble-rouser named Jesus of Nazareth.

While Jesus is flawless, our religious sensibilities—whether our doctrinal or ethical systems—are always subject to error. Thus they are only redeemable as they are made subject to Christ's constant transformation. And while Jesus contains the fullness of God, our knowledge of Him is limited by what we are able to receive at any given moment. God, being infinite, is more than any mortal can fully grasp. Thus there will always be more of Him in Christ to know and experience. But the end of existence is not understanding faith. It is living faith—a walk of utter dependence upon and loving attentiveness to Jesus Christ.

> Let your religion be less of a theory and more of a love affair.
> —G. K. Chesterton[12]

GOD'S SPIES

Two of the best lines Shakespeare ever wrote are these:

> And take upon's the mystery of things,
> As if we were God's spies.[13]

We who have been commissioned as *stewards* of the mystery must also be "spies" of the mystery. This is necessary if we are to both make sense of the mystery and manifest it.

Most people think of evil as a mystery. We believe the mystery of goodness, beauty, and truth is an even greater mystery than that of evil and wickedness. As one of "God's spies," are you always on the prowl to spy on the beauty, truth, and goodness Jesus is birthing in the world? For "God's spies," beauty, truth, and goodness are unlike the world's garbing of those categories. After all, Jesus is most beautiful at the ugliest moment of His life: His execution on the cross.

But the greatest and most magical mystery of all is the mystery of Christ Himself. The second great mystery is the church, which is His

> This is a great mystery.
> —Paul[14]

body. According to the New Testament, the mystery of God is Christ, and the mystery of Christ is the church.[15] The head and the body make up the one grand mystery of Scripture.

Ω

Paul loved talking about the mystery of Christ.[16] He even called Jesus "God's mystery," inviting us into "the knowledge of God's mystery, that is, Christ himself."[17] God's mystery is first and foremost the design of the holy Trinity to gather up[18] the whole of creation (all things in heaven and on earth) through Christ, having "made peace through the blood of His cross."[19]

Mystery is the heart of every relationship. When the mystery goes, there goes the romance and the passion. In every vital, living, dynamic relationship, the very best we can do is the mapping of each other's mystery. No matter how well you know someone, his or her mystery always deepens: for the whole is always greater than the sum of its parts.

There are basically two strategies that religion can employ when dealing with divine mystery: hide the mystery, or display the mystery through prayer, worship, art, and conversation. Byzantium and Eastern Christianity chose to display the mystery, whereas Western Christianity chose to hide it. But it even got worse. Beginning with Descartes, Western Christianity moved from "truth as mystery" to "truth as certainty."

WEARERS OF THE DUNCE CAP

Ever wonder where the "dunce cap" came from?

During the last years of the thirteenth century, the Franciscan friar Duns Scotus taught at Oxford. This philosophical theologian, dubbed "Doctor Subtilis" (the Subtle Doctor), was celebrated for being the most complex and clever of all the Oxford lecturers. He boasted an explanation for everything and often explained away everything. Because Duns Scotus was, in the words of his biographer, "the least likely to appeal to mystery and the most likely to solve a problem by intellectual gymnastics,"[20] he got the nickname "dimwit" and was mocked for being a "duns" (or dunce).

So the dunce cap emerged from a time when the mocking was directed at those who couldn't traffic in mystery, not at those who could.

When truth is encountered as certainty rather than mystery, open spaces of providence and possibility begin to close. The idea that you can discern truth by diagramming propositions or analyzing principles disenchants the world and "drawstrings" the heavens.[21] Only by living the mystery can truth be discovered.

This is not to say that we cannot be certain about anything.

Paul wrote, "We walk by faith, not by sight."[22] Faith is knowledge that transcends the realm of the physical senses. Hebrews 11:1 calls it the "evidence of things not seen." By faith, we know God. By faith, we touch the spiritual, invisible world. Faith is not mental assent or wishful thinking. It's another sense as real as our physical senses.

At the same time, the mystery of our faith opens the door for embracing paradox and even logical contradictions. Consequently, the phrase "It's a mystery" is not a starting base, but an ending gush. As G. K. Chesterton once put it, "The riddles of God are more satisfying than the solutions of man."[23]

Leonard had a godly mother who taught the Scriptures. When she got to a portion of Scripture that she couldn't understand, she would wrestle with it for a while, and if it still didn't yield understanding, she would smile and say, "Let's just put that verse into the mystery box."

But saying that God is a mystery can be a cop-out. When we don't understand something, it's quite easy to dismiss (or repress) it with, "Well, God moves in mysterious ways, doesn't He?" On the other hand, embracing mystery opens the door for appreciating how infinitely "beyond" all of us our Lord really is. It produces heart-awe mixed with a peaceful confidence in a God who is bigger than we can ever imagine.

> We must know God or perish. But unless we know God as ultimate mystery we do not know God at all.
> —Oxford scholar G. B. Caird[24]

To the person who walks in the Spirit, paradox, mystery, and uncertainty propel him forward instead of bogging him down. Those who live by faith can live in the presence of mystery and be motivated to rest in God's loving care. The person who walks by the physical senses alone, however, will be tempted to reject mystery—even though it's an essential part of the Christian faith. And this often leads to the frail and foolish attempt to explain a God who is beyond explanation.

> The more you know the more you know how little you know. Your frustration is finite and your ignorance is infinite. The more you resolve your frustration at your ignorance, and the more you repair the damage done in your life that led to your disappointment in your ignorance, the more you may be able to love your ignorance and woo it. All new will come from what you are ignorant of now.
>
> —Clifford Scott, "Who Is Afraid of Wilfred Bion?"[25]

One of the most powerful images of the Bible is Moses reaching out for more of God and only being able to see God's back side—[26] a reaching out for more of the divine echoed in the hemorrhaging woman's ability to reach out and touch only the hem of Jesus' garment.[27]

Two things we learn from these reaching-out episodes: (1) we are severely limited in what we can know; and (2) our reach can, at least, touch the fringe.

Moses' reach gave him the hunger for more—"I want to see

Your face, God." But God said, "No! You're not ready. You can't see it and live." So God doesn't give us His face. But He does give us His right hand—and its name is Jesus.

LIFE WILL FIND A WAY

The Christ who is truly (but only partially) present in our doctrine and experience is the true substance of the Christian faith. As for us, we will always "know in part" until we meet Him "face to face."[28] Concerning the reality of Christ Himself, all the fullness of God dwells within Him.[29]

It is for this reason that every theological system breaks down somewhere. Every systematic theology, no matter how coherent or logical, eventually meets some passage of Scripture or passage of life that refuses to fit into it. Such passages have to be bent, twisted, and forced to fit the system.

Why is this? It's because Christ is too immense, too imponderable, and too alive to be tied into any immovable system of thought constructed by finite humans.

Thus, He will always break out. As Jeff Goldblum's character said in the hit movie *Jurassic Park*—"Life will find a way." (That was his response to the idea that scientists had created an ironclad, airtight system to keep dinosaurs from reproducing.) Jesus Christ is too alive to be caged in any human system. As Paul exclaimed in holy exasperation, "How unsearchable are His judgments and His ways past finding out!"[30]

Life will find a way.

Jesus is not just one way, a better way, a pleasant way on a good day. He is *the* way.

Jesus is not just one truth, a higher truth, or a more personal truth. He is *the* truth.

Jesus is not just another life, a nicer life, a more abundant life. He is *the* life of God Himself.

> Without the Way,
> there is no going,
> Without the Truth,
> there is no knowing,
> Without the Life,
> there is no living.
> —Thomas à Kempis[31]

In short, following Jesus doesn't mean trying to create a weapons-grade theological system to analyze, explain, and contain Him. Neither does it mean trying to obey His teachings by the power of our own volition. When you say yes to Jesus, you are saying yes to a person, not to a proposition. Just as when you propose to your spouse, the proposal is not to propositions but to a human being. In vowing to be a disciple of Jesus, your "vow" is like any other vow of love in all of love's varieties. You pledge your allegiance not to the vows, but to the person you love. The padlock of wedlock is not the vows; it's the love. The padlock is a love-lock.

When you vow allegiance to Jesus, you are pledging allegiance to journey together without knowing everything about where you're headed, and without expecting everything to be spelled out in some prenuptial. But you do know with whom you want to travel through life.[32] And you know who the "head" of the relationship is.

So, Christianity is not an allegiance to a complex doctrinal or ethical system, but a passionate love for a way of living in the world that's rooted in living by Jesus, the way, the truth, and the life. Our theologies, doctrines, and subjective experiences are designed to flow organically from our loving relationship to Christ, but they are never to substitute for it.

WHAT DO YOU SEEK?

A few years ago, a Christian group visited the Soviet Union before the fall of the Berlin wall. When the guide who was showing the Christians around Leningrad came to a statue of Lenin, the guide paused and said reflectively, "You Christians have a great message, but we Communists will win the world. Christ means something to you. Communism means everything to us."

The great Methodist evangelist and missionary E. Stanley Jones visited Soviet Russia in the later years of his life and came away with a different opinion. He was visibly shaken by the Communists' dedication and party loyalty. *They're building their society, and they seem unstoppable,* he thought, *but their kingdom is built on force. I belong to a kingdom built on faith. Their foundation is shakable. The foundation of God's kingdom is unshakable.*

> A religion without mystery must be a religion without God.
> —Anglican clergyman Jeremy Taylor (1613–1667)[33]

Jones's ensuing book, *The Unshakable Kingdom and the Unchanging Person* (1972), predicted that Communism would fall shortly, and he called on Christians to become an unshakable force in giving their allegiance to an "unchanging person"—Jesus Christ—whose "kingdom is forever" and who is our "all and in all."[34] Similarly, Paul wrote to the Corinthian church, "I determined not to know anything among you except Jesus Christ and Him crucified."[35]

Maybe enough "battle fatigue" has set in that the body of Christ is finally at the place where it is less interested in fighting those who oppose it and more interested in nurturing the faith it believes in and lives by. Perhaps the time has come for us to focus on the "real thing." What do you seek?

Do you seek righteousness? Jesus Christ is righteousness and sanctification.[36]

Do you seek wisdom? His name is Jesus.[37]

Do you desire peace? Jesus Christ is peace.[38]

Do you want truth? That's what Jesus is.[39]

Do you seek the power of God? Jesus Christ *is* the power of God.[40]

Christ is the embodiment of all that God desires to give His children—both His teachings and His virtues.

Wisdom, peace, truth, righteousness, beauty, grace, mercy, love, kindness, patience, and goodness are just words that were forced into existence to describe aspects of Him.

May we, therefore, stop seeking "things" and instead lay hold of the "real thing"—Jesus. He is the razor edge of truth, the road that leads us out of the ditch.

> *Sing and rejoice, O daughter Zion!*
> *For lo, I will come and dwell in your midst.*
>
> —Zechariah 2:10 NRSV

CHAPTER 6

HIS FACE OR YOUR FACE?

S omeone who is a part of our Twitter communities posted this tweet not too long ago: "There is no greater cause that you can give your life to than the cause of Christ." Hmm . . . So Christ is now a "cause"? Jesus has become just another cause among many, one more cause to support on Facebook, or another celebrity to be a fan of?

Indeed, it's possible to confuse the "cause" of Christ with the person of Christ. Yet when the early church said, "Jesus is Lord," they did *not* mean "Jesus is my *cause*" or "Jesus is my core value."

Regarding values, in our public school systems, "character development" is passé because nothing "moral" or "universal" can be taught. Reigning politically correct[1] orthodoxies mandate that all people be respected for their own truths. What has replaced "character development" is "cause development," where even the very young are being taught to embrace some "cause" in the hopes that those causes can give them some sense of meaning and purpose to life.

Several popular causes current in our schools are: getting rid of disposable plates in the cafeteria and using real plates, global warming, and fighting for gay marriage. Parents cheer our schools to continue "cause development" because it appears that having a cause is an acceptable substitute for having character.

This culture loves causes, and it lionizes those who died fighting them. There is nothing wrong with causes. Archbishop Oscar Romero took up the cause of victims displaced in the Salvadoran civil war, and was assassinated during his homily as he was giving mass in 1980. Now "San Romero," as he is often called, is one of only ten twentieth-century martyrs honored above the Great West Door of Westminster Abbey in London. On the other hand, Brother Roger Schutz, founder of Taizé, was killed on August 16, 2005, not for a cause he was promoting, but because of who he was—a follower of Jesus.[2]

Jesus isn't a cause; He is a real and living person who can be known, loved, experienced, enthroned, and embodied. Focusing on His cause or mission doesn't equate with focusing on or following Him. It's all too possible to serve the "god" of serving Jesus as opposed to serving Him out of an enraptured heart that's been captivated by His irresistible beauty and unfathomable love. But Jesus led us to think of God differently, as relationship, as the God of all relationship.

To reduce Jesus to a cause may be a symptom of what some scholars call the "Ephesus Syndrome." Of the seven cities addressed in Revelation 2 and 3, the church in Ephesus probably faced the greatest social, political, and theological challenges. The

Lord Jesus praised the Ephesian church for resisting the lure of empire and for its vigilance in brandishing numerous causes. Yet in the midst of lavish praise for the church's persistence and perseverance, the Ephesian Christians were rebuked for abandoning the love they had at first.[3] In their zeal for theological purity and social relevance, they lost their "first love"—the sovereign Christ and the supremacy of loving Him.

WHAT IS GOD DOING?

Part of the problem of defining Christ as a "cause" is that it fails to make the question of "What are you doing?" part of the larger question, "What is God doing?" If we take seriously the reality that we can simultaneously *follow* and *fall in* with Christ, then we, together with the other parts of His body, *are* Christ. "As He is, so are we in this world," John wrote.[4]

This is what we mean when we speak of incarnating Jesus. We're not simply talking about doing the tasks that Jesus would have done when He physically walked in and around Capernaum, or taking up causes He might have taken up if He were still walking planet Earth today. We are talking about living in a unique Christ/you, "I am" relationship.

That means, for instance, that two different followers of Christ who are both incarnating their living relationship with Christ may be fully in God's will while engaging in causes that may counter one another. For instance, one Christ-follower could be involved in a life of military service while a second Christ-follower could be engaged in aiding the very people the first is fighting.

One of the subtle but insidious problems of WWJD (the

"What would Jesus do?" question[5]) is the assumption of a single Christian response for every situation. For this to be so, the WWJD question would need to be phrased something like, "What would Jesus the incarnate Son of God, the first-century artisan-turned-itinerant-preacher and Savior of the universe do in this situation?" because Jesus the Galilean man is not God's person for your situation. No, the incarnate Christ in you *is* God's person for your situation. Consequently, the question is not "What would Jesus do?" but "What does Jesus want to do now through me . . . through us?"

Being Jesus for the world does not mean that Christ has come to obliterate you. It rather means that Christ has come to complete you and to live His resurrection life through you. Granted, Jesus Christ has crucified your flesh and the old fallen humanity that gave birth to it. But you have been resurrected with Christ, and you are a new creature, part of the new humanity of which Jesus is the firstborn son.

Perichoresis is a composite Greek word that every Christian should know. It means "move about" or "dance around." The Cappadocian Fathers used it to define the communion of the Trinity as the "Great Dance." Father, Son, and Holy Spirit flow and frame their lives in a dance of perfect love, and we are invited to add our moves to this dance of the divine. A *perichoretic* relationship is one where we draw life and energy from this dance with the divine life. Christians have a *perichoretic* relationship with Christ. That relationship makes you more fully yourself than you could have ever been apart from Him.

The gospel is not the eradication of you; it is not self-negation. Rather, the gospel is the radical reconfiguration of the "self" within a relational context.[6] The old self has been put to death, and the new self in Christ has taken its place. And your new self is the real "you."[7] Christ has supplanted us!

If Christ is fully in me (Leonard) and I am fully in Christ, then I will be living fully as Len. The same with Frank and the same with you. We live out the real essence of our humanity only when we are walking in Jesus Christ, who is the quintessential human.

> The Christian faith has only one object: the mystery of Christ dead and risen. But this unique mystery subsists under different modes: it is prefigured in the Old Testament, it is accomplished historically in the earthly life of Christ, it is contained in mystery in the sacraments, it is lived mystically in souls, it is accomplished socially in the Church, it is consummated eschatologically in the heavenly kingdom.
>
> —Jean Danielou[8]

As such, the Lord helps us become more "rounded" human beings—not more straight-edged, straightlaced, straight-backed, straight-faced, straightjacketed human copies, but more "rounded," more complete and whole humans. Jesus is God's original thought for humanity. He is the paragon of humanness, and all who are in Him and share His life are part of the new humanity that He has brought into existence through His resurrection.

This will lead each of us to do life differently, even from other followers of Christ. Can the same Christ allow one person to be a

Calvinist while permitting another to be an Arminian? The answer is yes. This is why the life of Christ has a freedom, a specificity, a range of reach that truly takes the breath away as it girdles the globe. The truth is, most Calvinists live like Arminians (they hold themselves and others responsible for their actions). And most Arminians pray like Calvinists (they submit their requests to the will of God).

LIVING BEYOND OURSELVES

One of the most amazing but least noticed features of the New Testament portrayal of Jesus is its lack of interest in what Jesus looked like or His personality quirks. For example, what did Jesus' face look like? The Gospels don't tell. What they showcase is the way His face was spat upon, blindfolded, smitten, bruised for our sakes—all without any retaliation.

It is almost as if Jesus does not live out of Himself, but beyond Himself ("I and My Father are one;"[9] "As the Father has sent Me;"[10] "As the Father loved Me;"[11] "The Son can do nothing by himself. He does only what he sees the Father doing."[12]). Jesus less revealed who He is than who God the Father is, and what is beyond Him. For example, here is the message Mary was given for the apostles: "Go . . . and say to them, 'I am ascending to my Father and your Father, to my God and your God.'"[13] How amazing is this? Jesus was saying that because of His resurrection and ascension, we share in His sonship with God; we have shared privileges with Him.

Jesus' sense of self is God-centered, not self-centered. Nothing He does is in the service of self, but in the service of God. The essence of Jesus' being is not His; He is continually receiving it from the Father. He lives in a state of *empathy*,[14] in which one steps out of himself, which is the beginning of compassion, and steps into the sandals of others.

Could it be that those who are remade in Christ's image live in a similar fashion? We do not live from within but from beyond; we do not live out of ourselves, but beyond ourselves. How did Paul put it? "It is no longer I who live, but it is Christ who lives in me."[15] So for a Christian to say, "I am" is to utter something quite profound, even self-contradictory.

In John Milton's classic *Paradise Lost*, satan declares himself to be "self-begot, self-raised."[16] That is satan's greatest lie and his greatest delusion—the delusion that lies behind a great deal of human disaster: the myth that we are self-made and self-raised. By means of every medium imaginable and every merchant of materialism (which are really merchants of the self), the evil one perpetuates the fantasy that we are self-begotten; he promotes our forgetting that it is God who has made us, and not we ourselves. The old cynicism that says that Americans hold nothing sacred is challenged by the realization that we do hold something sacred: the individual, the self.

Is your faith based more on a flaccid "What's in it for me?" than on pursuing your Lord and the concerns that He has?

Then turn your head away from the reflective pool before you drown in Narcissus Nirvana. Get outside of yourself and into Christ. In this way you will live beyond yourself to see others, not just yourself, and in seeing them you find yourself. (Maybe we need some "Drown Narcissus" rituals . . . like a fast from "self-help groups"—a favorite oxymoron—or self-help books.)

Garrison Keillor says that there are only two ways to cure our "raging narcissism": (1) have children, or (2) move to a foreign country where people don't care who you are or what you do.[17]

But Jesus says that there's another way to cure our "raging narcissism:" starve our inner narcissist by forgetting ourselves and focusing on God.

Our problem is this: we have even created a narcissistic form of Christianity, in which "conversion" is less a turning toward Christ than a turning toward success or fame or fortune. Narcissus never had it so good than in best-seller Christianity, which has become self-centeredness wrapped up as "spirituality," which has become the latest fashion accessory for the person who has everything. A survey of the Christian Book Association's best-selling books as we began the twenty-first century found that family and parenting topics accounted for nearly half of the titles, with the rest focused mainly on the self.[18] Of the top 100 books, just 6 were about the Bible, 4 were about Jesus, and 3 were about evangelism. "The Christianity of the bestseller lists tends to be personal, private, and interior," wrote Gene Edward Veith, "with little attention to theology or to the church."[19]

We have made conversion primarily about ourselves, a finding of ourselves and a fulfilling of ourselves. We've made it a journey of self-discovery rather than a journey of God discovery. Yet conversion is not about us, but about God's overture of love, without which we are devoid of sufficient motive or power to change and be changed. True "conversion" is to lay hold of Christ, or rather, as Paul corrected himself, to allow Christ to lay hold of us.[20] True "conversion" is directed toward the one to whom we convert, the one to whom we turn. It is a life of "fullness," in which the "fullness" is Christ.

You are not the point. And we are not the point. Jesus Christ always has been and always will be the point. All the arrows point to Him and not to us.

Some reading those words may say, "Of course Jesus is the point. What Christian doesn't know that?" Well, Frank recently spoke at a conference and shared on the unsearchable riches of Christ. One person responded by saying, "I've been a Christian for over thirty years. I've been a worship leader, taught Sunday school, and was very active in ministry from the day I believed on Jesus. I've served in some very large nondenominational, evangelical, Bible-believing churches. And for the first time in my life I now realize that it's all about Christ. This message is not being preached today."

This sort of response is very common when a believer gets a fresh glimpse from the Holy Spirit as to who Jesus really is in the purpose of God.

Robert F. Taft, perhaps the world's leading scholar of Byzantine liturgy, compares the worldview behind Byzantine art and architecture to the twenty-first-century worldview:

> Unlike in the past, people nowadays do not see themselves as finding their place in a scheme of things larger and—yes— more important than themselves. On the contrary, they see the larger reality in terms of how they can exploit it for their own self-fulfilment.[21]

WHAT SHALL YOU DO?

So in light of all that we've just shared with you, what should you do?

Here's our answer: Get a fresh glimpse of your incomparable Lord, and you will be emboldened to stop spending your life on yourself. Connect with Him who is life, and you will be empowered to deny yourself, live beyond yourself, and live outside yourself. Let go, break free of the self, the captivity of *me*. Only Christ can set you free from yourself—the old self that He nailed to His cross. No amount of willpower or good intention can accomplish this. So lay hold of Him and escape the straitjacket of the exalted, exaggerated, narcissistic sense of self. You and your causes are *not* the center of the universe. You are part of a process of life that is greater than you. The self only exists at all inasmuch as it participates in the being of God. You are not the main character in your own story. God in Christ is.

There is no "Secret" any longer. The "Secret" is out.[22] That which has been kept hidden has now been revealed: "Christ in you, the hope of glory."[23] The secret of the Secret is that to find your life, to live the best life you can live, you have to give your life away.

"You want to find your life? Then lose it," Jesus said. Lose it on others. Do you want to "manifest" something? Then manifest Christ, the fullness of the Spirit. Jesus is in the self-transcending, *not* the self-fulfilling, business.

Pope John Paul II's word to the faithful as Christianity entered its third millennium was this: "Contemplate the face of Christ."[24] It's a word for every minute, not just a new millennium.

Today, we behold the face of Christ in a spiritual way. As Peter said, even though we have not seen Him physically, we love Him.[25] Paul went further by saying that we behold the face of Christ as in a mirror, and by that beholding, we are changed into His image.[26]

The best place to see our Lord's face is when we are on our faces.

As Gerard Manley Hopkins (1844–89) said in one of the few sermons that he didn't destroy, "There met in Jesus Christ all that can make man lovely and loveable."[27] And truly, "In Him dwells all the fullness of the Godhead bodily."[28]

And because Jesus fully dwells in His body today, we meet the face of Christ in our Christian sisters and brothers. Just as Paul said, we do not know Christ after the flesh, but we know Him as part of the new creation.[29] And that new creation is the church, which is His body.

Consequently, in a world more concerned about following a program or a cause than following Christ, in a world where life is lived in beta, we must focus on Christ—not the dead Jesus, but the living Christ, and not the Christ in art, but the breathing Christ that becomes art in you and me. For only in that face can we find ourselves. Only in the face of Christ can we be freed from the facades of our own making.

In 2004 Jean-François Rivest, the French conductor of the Montreal symphony, with only thirty-six hours' advance notice, was called in to conduct a major concert of the Toronto symphony. He was such a success with everyone involved (especially the musicians) and on short notice displayed such confidence that there was a chorus of "How did you do it?"

His response went like this: "Yes, I have confidence in my abilities, but it is more than that. I love the music, and I love the musicians who devote their lives to the music. So I always start by forming a relationship with the musicians (even in twelve hours or less), and sometimes it happens, sometimes not. But when we all start experiencing together the music, it is beautiful, rich, inspiring.

"When I hear the burning passion of the individual musician for the music, then I try to create enough safety for the musicians to express themselves. And together we come to a common understanding of the interpretation of the music. So, it's not me. I'm not the cause. Neither are the musicians. It's the music—it is the music—that brings us all together to work its magic."[30]

And it is Jesus who brings all the instruments together to work His magic.

CHAPTER 7

A COLLISION OF TWO EMPIRES

Jesus Christ has never been a social activist or a moral philosopher. To pitch Him that way is to drain His glory and dilute His excellence. While justice is important, justice apart from Christ is a dead thing. The only battering ram that can storm the gates of hell is not the cry of justice, but the name of Jesus. Jesus Christ is the embodiment of justice, peace, holiness, righteousness, and every other virtue.

Christ is the sum of all spiritual things, the "strange attractor" of the cosmos. When Jesus becomes an abstraction, faith loses its reproductive power. "Jesus did not come to make bad people good. He came to make dead people live."[1]

Paul said that Jesus is "head over all things [for] the church."[2] Notice, Jesus is head over all things not for the state but for the church. All things are placed under His feet, Paul wrote, but Jesus has been appointed "head" of "all things" for the *church*." Some have

105

made Jesus the chaplain of the American dream. Others have made Him the chaplain of the Democratic Party. Still others have made Jesus the chaplain of capitalism and Republicanism. All are equally blasphemous. Most blasphemous of all are those who would decapitate the head from its body and render Christ irrelevant.

> *There's a wideness in God's mercy,*
> *Like the wideness of the sea;*
> *There's a kindness in His justice,*
> *Which is more than liberty.*
>
> —Frederick William Faber[3]

REFRAMING THE KINGDOM

Some today teach that the kingdom of God is a political utopia taught by Jesus that we Christians are charged to bring about. This is essentially the old-fashioned "social gospel." Those who hold this view are still caught up in the old "fundamentalist individual gospel" versus "social gospel" dichotomy. Advocates think that the only way to talk about social justice is to do it in social gospel terms.

We do not reject Jesus, or justice, or the kingdom. But we reject the notion that you can take the justice side of Christ and push it into a separate theme on its own. Origen said that Jesus is the *autobasilia*. He is, in Himself, the kingdom. As the stories were told, "entering the kingdom" became the favorite metaphor for experiencing Christ. Jesus' own person and work are the establishing of a new humanity—a new social form of existence. In Him, we find the kingdom of God. In Him, we find what freedom and equality genuinely mean. Practically speaking, the church (when she is functioning properly) is the new society that Jesus is creating. Christ and the church cannot be separated.

To put it in Bonhoeffer's terms, God is both Act and Being,[4] and the act and being of God are found in Christ. He is God's Act and God's Being. It's a royal mistake to separate the two.

A good definition of the kingdom of God is as follows: *the manifestation of God's ruling presence.* "The kingdom of God is in the midst of you," Jesus said. In other words, Jesus was saying, "I'm standing here in your midst. I am the kingdom incarnated. Not only in what I do, but in who I am."

The kingdom of God is made visible when the community of the King embodies justice, peace, and love together and then shares it with the world. The church, therefore, is the embodiment and instrument for displaying the kingdom of God.

The stripping of Jesus from His kingdom is a little like the wording Harvard stripped from its motto. Harvard's current motto "*Veritas,*" or Truth, used to be a mite different. The university's original motto was "*Veritas pro Christo et ecclesia,*" or "Truth for Christ and his Church." Truth is more powerful than lies. The power of truth remains, even if truth is not followed. But real Truth is a Person. Truth comes to us now, as it always has, through the Holy Spirit, who is the Spirit of Truth who brings that which is true to life in our lives. Truth is also always in line with Scripture, for the same Spirit who makes truth come alive has breathed upon the written Word.

We must never avoid social issues. But the distinctive mark of a Christian is that you don't begin with a social or moral issue.

You begin with God. You start with God's revelation in Jesus, and the relationship of justifying/sanctifying/glorifying grace that the "heir of all things"[5] releases in all of us. You make the Light of the World, not culture, your reference point. Our time should be spent figuring out our relationship to Jesus, and what He is doing in the world. Why? So we can join Him in what He's already doing. If we start anywhere else but Christ, we lose our way. If we start with the social and political as our reference point, the "social gospel" becomes very much "social" and very little "gospel." In truth, there is no "gospel" that is not a "social gospel."

> The preferential option for the poor is implicit in Christological faith.
> —Pope Benedict XVI[6]

For example, when we reach out to the poor and sick, we are not doing so because of some principle of justice, or some theology of poverty and sickness, or some political platform or legislation, or some responsible way of dealing with surplus wealth. We do so for three reasons:

1. The deepest hungers of the human heart are for forgiveness and reconciliation with God.
2. We are reaching out to Jesus Himself ("I was sick and you visited Me"[7]). In the poor and sick, it is Christ whom we attend and feed and love. Followers of Jesus exist for others, not for themselves.
3. The life of Christ within us compels us to reach out to such. The Galilean prophet who healed the sick and cared for the poor continues His ministry in and through us today.

This reframing of "the poor" was one of the greatest contributions of Christianity. The pagan world called poor people "base and shady." The Christians called them "sisters and brothers," and identified them with Christ. The "needy" and "afflicted" received more than alms; they also received prayer and affection and relationship. The poor were not a political problem. The poor were "us," not "them."[8] Care of the poor is a matter of orthodox faith.

The story of redemption is where we begin talking about moral and social issues. Of course, it is one thing to get the *meaning* of what Jesus said and did; it is another thing to start *meaning it*. Meaning is meaningless until and unless you start "*meaning it*." In the same way, respiration is composed of inspiration (breathing in the meaning) and exhalation (living out the "meaning it"). To do only one or the other is called expiration.

But "meaning it" means something other than politicization. The pressure on the church to "pietize" politics and mumble polite noises in political directions will only get stronger. What happens when these siren songs are heeded is evident in any reading of the history of the church, where the worst in the history of politics is on display. The perversion of the best yields the worst.

Cambridge historian Eamon Duffy visited the National Gallery's "Seeing Salvation" exhibit (2000), which makes both of us jealous. The earliest symbolic representation of Christ he could find on display was the Chi-Rho monogram, encoding the opening letters of the name "Christ" in Greek. Duffy found the monogram on the reverse of a coin the emperor Constantine struck in 327, fourteen years after seizing control of the Roman Empire by force. On this coin, Christ's name halos a war banner bearing the inscription "The hope of the State." Duffy comments, "From the very beginning, Christian art was hijacked to serve the powerful and the successful."[9]

It is a Christian's fatal conceit to think he can bring in the kingdom. A careful reading of the Scriptures reveals that the kingdom is not something that we bring, or build, or cause, or create. The kingdom is a presence that we enter, a gemlike gift that we receive and treasure, a new creation that engulfs and embraces us. In other words, the kingdom of God is Jesus the Christ, and His righteousness. In seeking Him, "all these things [are] added"[10] in our lives.

> "Surely goodness and mercy will follow . . ."
> —Psalm 23

RETHINKING JUSTICE

We have learned a lot from different perspectives on Jesus: feminist theology, creation theology, process theology, liberation theology, narrative theology, postliberal theology, emergent theology. But when the business of the church becomes more about pursuing the "reign of God" than following Jesus, then we start hearing more about justice than justification, and Jesus the Liberator replaces Jesus the Way, the Truth, the Life.[11] He, in fact, is all of those things.

The person who invented the "wiki" software in 1994, Jimmy Wales, confessed that his ambition was very simple: "Imagine a world where every single person is given free access to the sum of all human knowledge. That's what we're doing [by creating the

Wiki software]."[12] No, that's what God has already done. Its name is not Wikipedia. *His* name is Emmanuel.

We find the current linkage of "kingdom" and "justice" problematic for a couple of reasons. First, the language of "justice" is the language of the prosecution. Operation Enduring Freedom, launched in October 2001 to avenge 9/11, was first known by another name: Operation Infinite Justice. The church now seems to have a similar name: Operation Justice.

When did the church become part of the prosecution and not the defense? Is the church reflecting a cultural fixation that has moved from defense attorney (*Perry Mason* and *Matlock*) to district attorney (*Law & Order* or *CSI*)? Besides, since when did law have to do with justice? Law has to do with legislation, with power, with the politics of empire. Granted, there are times when the church should stand up prophetically and speak to power, saying, "This is wrong because it outrages the image of God in human beings." Slavery, sex trafficking, genocide, abortion, etc., are some of those issues. But such ministry is not what the church specializes in.

Don't misunderstand. We are not arguing for a highly privatized, individual, pietistic relationship with Jesus that rules out any social aspects of the gospel. Our relationship with Christ has intense public and social dimensions. But the social and political reform of the world through the powers that be has never been the agenda of the body of Christ. Caesar sought to change the hearts of men by laws and institutions. Jesus changes the hearts of women and men and brings them into a new society, the church, the firstfruits of a new creation.

In the ancient Roman courtroom, the defense was usually

seen as the more honorable trade. The early church was deeply ambivalent about whether a Christian could even serve as a judge without putting his soul in peril. A follower of Jesus seated on some elevated throne, dispensing justice, seemed not to be in keeping with Jesus' injunction "Judge not." Christianity is rooted in a Passion narrative in which the worst was done not by wicked people, but by good people in cahoots with district attorneys and justice departments. Jesus was executed not by some frenzied mob or rogue justice, but by the best religion, the most powerful state, and the most perfect legal system, functioning as they were each designed to do. We're not sure that Rousseau was right when he said that the more you think, the less you feel. But we are sure that the more you judge, the less you love.

Second, when "justice" becomes a goal in itself, or God is equated with justice, then we have moved from Christianity to another religion. The most radical Shi'i writers in Iran have been talking in a very secular way about the return of the Madhi (Hidden Imam) signaling the reign of "justice" that an Islamic revolution in an Islamic republic must establish. This "justice" will not come from God, but is essentially a replacement for Him; and their concept of justice uses religious forms and arguments to disguise a monochromic concept of an earthly social, economic, political system in which no one will have authority over anyone else. Everyone will dress alike, have the exact same housing, and be alike in every other way. The Koran professes to be the Word made text. Jesus is the Word made flesh.

> Peace on earth, and mercy mild, God and sinners reconciled.
> —Charles Wesley[13]

Third, the "love of justice" and the "hunger for justice" betray a misreading of Micah 6:8, where we are to love mercy, do justice, and walk humbly. We have too many people loving *justice* when they should be loving *mercy*—and *doing* justice.

You may have heard the story of the woman who went to have her picture taken and said to the photographer, "Try to do me justice." And the photographer said to his assistant, "What this woman needs is not justice, but mercy."

We do too. We can live only by mercy, not by justice. In the interplay of law and grace, we count on grace. We don't follow the law exactly, unless a police officer is watching. We expect grace. And we tread far in the land of grace when we drive, or when we cross the street, or even when we play baseball, softball, and six-man football. It reminds us of the old "mercy rule," which goes like this: after half-time, if you're behind by more than 45 points, you can stop the game so the other team isn't humiliated. The mercy rule is used especially where there is no game clock and play could continue ad nauseam. Unfortunately, it is seldom used in competitive sports beyond the high school level.

We guarantee you one thing: all those today who are clamoring, hungering, and seeking for justice will one day sing a very different tune. When we present ourselves before our Creator and Judge, it will not be "I've given my life to the struggle for justice. Now it's my turn. Give it to me! Give me justice." Any takers?

"Having faith" is less a knowledge of God's justice than trust in God's mercy. Christians want to live just lives, but we are justified not by works; we're justified by grace. Grace alone saves. The redemption story features the promise that where evil abounds, grace abounds more. God doesn't judge our lives in terms of our performance or success or length of service. All that matters in the end is the freewheeling generosity and audacious mercy of God. That's why whenever Jesus metes out justice, it turns out to be an unjust justice, a bending of the letter of the law to the spirit of the law. That's also why Jesus' promises in the Beatitudes don't come with conditions, like "Blest are the hungry who follow me" or "Blest are the faithful who give generously." There are no strings. The hungry, the poor, the sorrowing, all receive God's mercy without conditions, without any strings attached.

> Christ is crucified by the priests of the purest religion of his day and by the minions of the justest, the Roman Law. The fanaticism of the priests is the fanaticism of all good men, who do not know that they are not as good as they esteem themselves. The complacence of Pilate represents the moral mediocrity of all communities, however just.
>
> —Reinhold Niebuhr[14]

REDISCOVERING MERCY

The Hebrew word for mercy is *hesed*, and justice is *mishpat*. In the Old Testament, they are opposite sides of the same coin, although *hesed* is used more than any other word in the Bible to describe God's love for us. But in the New Testament, they both are expressions of God's love, where mercy trumps justice. What first-century rabbinic literature called God's "two measures," justice (*mishpat*) and mercy (*hesed*), were brought together on the cross, and all previous perceptions of justice turned upside down.

Grace gives us what we do not deserve; mercy delivers us from what we do deserve.

The Christian tradition refuses to separate love and justice. In fact, for Jesus, love may be the theological name for justice. Throughout the New Testament, justice gets swept up in righteousness, and both are swallowed up in love. According to Greek scholar Spiros Zodhiates,[15] the root of both the Greek words for "justice" and "righteousness" refers to treating others according to their "character, function, and purpose" to achieve "harmony and congruity." Is that not a good definition of love?

In Mary's "Magnificat,"[16] it was God's mercy, not His justice, that performed the mighty deeds in the song. God's mercy "scattered the proud," "put down the mighty from their thrones," and "exalted the lowly." And the mercy of God is what "filled the hungry with good things" but sent the rich away empty. The distinctive sign of God's mercy? It turns the tables on earthly power and prestige, and it elevates the least and the last.

Jesus was known not for His love of justice but for His love of mercy: "Blessed are the merciful," He said, "for they shall obtain mercy."[17] And again, "Be merciful, just as your Father also is merciful."[18] In the parable of the unforgiving servant, Jesus urges us to show mercy to those who sin against us.[19] In fact, this theme is so strong that in *Palm Sunday*, Kurt Vonnegut claimed that mercy is the only good idea that has been introduced into the world thus far.[20]

The Jesus Prayer is one of the treasures of the Orthodox Church, which these sisters and brothers believe sums up the gospel: "Lord Jesus Christ, Son of God, have mercy on me, a sinner."

The Orthodox repeat the Jesus Prayer over and over again in the course of a day.

Part of the struggle against injustice is to stop the passive consumption of culture and to enflesh faith in the hands and faces of mercy and love. Christians should be active participants in making and evangelizing this "recombinant culture"[21] that is increasingly susceptible to "Rip. Mix. Burn"[22] initiatives. But we do not aim to make it into a "Christian culture," but a human culture that is merciful and hospitable to all humanity. We would be wise to remember that the best we can do is change the world; only Jesus can *save*

the world. Jesus' name means exactly who He is: "God saves." The mission of Jesus is the redemption of the human race and the bringing forth of a new creation.

> See, I return good for evil, love for injuries, and for deeper wounds a deeper love.
>
> —the crucified Christ's message to the world, as written in the fifth century by Father Peter Chrysologus[23]

The current understanding of justice assumes freedom from suffering. In fact, there is a prevalent assumption that it is our just right to have no suffering or pain and, if we suffer, it is inherently unjust. Jesus Himself confronted this in the famous exchange with Peter in Mark 8.[24]

But crucified beauty, crucified goodness, crucified truth are God's notions of justice. The kingdom of God is the reign of mercy and compassion and shalom (peace), which is about right relationships in the midst of all that brings suffering. Justice does not assume freedom from suffering. After all, it was God's relational being that led to the creation of an imperfect world— one of pain and sickness and death. A perfect world would not have been God's companion, only His automaton. A "just world" would have been God's self-reflection—with no rejection, but no romance either; with no betrayal, but also no freedom.

Philosopher John MacMurray, in his Gifford Lectures at Glasgow in the mid-twentieth century, which made such an impression on future prime minister Tony Blair, made this comparison: "The maxim of illusory religion runs: 'Fear not; trust in God and he will see that none of the things you fear will happen to you'; that of real religion, on the contrary, is: 'Fear not, the things that you are afraid of are quite likely to happen to you, but they are nothing to be afraid of.'"[25]

Jesus doesn't offer us perfect health and massive wealth. What He does offer us is eternal life and a relationship with Himself, in which nothing can separate us from God's love. Followers of the Root of David[26] are like bent, gnarled trees on the Oregon coast. The south wind warms them; the gray sunshine nourishes them; the mists of rain and fog fertilize them; and the cold winter winds toughen them.

When the church confronts moments of *status confessionis*, when the church must speak a "Thus says the Lord" on politics, the suffering will increase, not diminish. But these moments of *status confessionis* are rare, and their very rarity makes them more powerful, so when the church does speak, people listen. The meaning of Christianity does not come from allegiance to principles of justice or complex theological doctrines, but from a passionate love for a way of living in the world that revolves around following Jesus, who taught that love is what makes life a success; not wealth or health or anything else. Only love.

Christians don't follow Christianity. They follow Christ. Jesus believed that the purpose of the Law was to structure a way of living together that He called "love." It is not law versus love. Rather, it is law *of* love. The main theme in the preaching of Jesus was that life with the Father was all about love.

A POLITICAL MESSIAH?

The principal weapon of our warfare against the powers and principalities of this world is not counter principles or propositions or political platforms or "Christian" legislation or electing the "right" political officials. It is Truth . . . and we seem more concerned about implementing the social implications of the gospel than the gospel itself, the fruit of which is to create a kingdom community that will demonstrate God's rule on earth.

Christians have a lover's quarrel with the world. Too many Christians want to change the world, not because they love the world but because they hate the world. The test of love's radiance: does it both transcend and embrace the world? We do not suggest as some do that the church's "justice mantras" are little more than socialist nuggets honeyed with Christian sweetness. But we do suggest that the widespread hunger for perfect justice is a reflection of the longing for lost meaning that can only be found in the One who "fills all in all."[27] Our "hunger for justice" is best turned into a hunger for the Just One,[28] and going deeper in Him and in relationship with others.

The Holy One's[29] public ministry began only after He faced and outfaced three temptations. The most tantalizing of the three was the temptation to turn the kingdom of God into a political program. Jesus shook off the lure of political theology by stiff-arming it with these words: "My kingdom is not of this world."[30]

What if Jesus had given in to the devil's temptation and accepted the riches, the kingdoms, the power? What would He have been today? A great king? A president? The head of the UN? Jesus' revolution was not about politics: He was *not* a political revolutionary. His revolution was a relational one in which He Himself would be Sword[31] and Shield.[32] Jesus didn't choose the primacy of the powers of religion/politics or the powers of the individual; He chose a third way—His indwelling presence experienced and displayed through a community of followers who embody the kingdom of God in their corporate life together.

This is why the Jewish establishment rejected Jesus' messiahship then, and Jewish scholars continue to critique his messianic claims today: the Messiah was supposed to gather Jewish exiles in Judea, overthrow the Roman oppressors, and establish a just kingdom on earth. Jesus did none of these things.[33] To accept Jesus was, according to Paul, to admit that Jewish law was obsolete and that a "new covenant" with God was possible.

While Jesus wasn't political in the modern sense of the word, He was political in this sense: Christ was the beginning of the change of the world. He inaugurated a new creation. And He showed us how prayer might set us on the right road to peace before politics.

As John Howard Yoder and Stanley Hauerwas have pointed out,[34] among other authors, the church is a new *polis*. It is a God-created community that embodies a new politic and new definitions of leadership. The church, therefore, is a colony from another realm, representing the rights of its sovereign Lord. So our politics are embodied in the life that we're called to live out together as God's people—as the church.

In this sense, the church is the new order. We are the beginning of God's kingdom that is already happening in the midst of the old order. If the church is operating properly in a given locality, the kingdom of God is seen. Justice, peace, love, mutual care, and giving, are made visible. Christ is seen on the earth again.

The church's claim on the future, therefore, is not a political one. If we are going to have a world at peace, we will need more than politics. We will need the Prince of Peace living through a community that embodies His nature. Again, the church is the true *polis* intended by God for all of humanity.

For that reason, a social order based on justice and peace cannot be established by human effort alone. Perfect peace and justice are works of divine grace in the hearts of those who respond to Christ's love. The kingdomization of any political platform is a form of uniting church and state, with unhealthy consequences for both. When the Spirit of Christ lives in you, you seldom end up following the political categories of any power structure, as if there were only a single "God's politics" or the church were "God's party."

In politics, everything is played out in the moral register—in the language of right and wrong. In faith, everything is played out in the relational register—in the language of vine and branches, living and dead, members and the dismembered. The final goal for anything new is not justice; it is life. Does this deserve to exist? Does it promote beauty, truth, goodness? When you stop dreaming for yourself and you start dreaming for God and the gospel, then "Thy kingdom come, Thy will be done on earth as it is in heaven."

Disciples of Jesus are troubled but not taken unawares by human depravity.

CONCLUSION

At the Italian Eucharistic Congress in Bologna in 1997, Cardinal Ratzinger fought having Bob Dylan sing before the pope. In his 2007 book *John Paul II, My Beloved Predecessor*, Ratzinger says he "doubts to this day whether it was right to let this kind of so-called prophet take the stage."[35] In Christmas 2009, both Dylan and the current pope went head to head on the charts for their Christmas albums. Geffen Records released a collection of litanies and chants sung by Pope Benedict, and Dylan released his first Christmas album.

But what John Paul II did was not so much to feature Bob Dylan but to use Dylan's music to make a point: he chose "Blowin' in the Wind" and said this: "You ask me how many roads a man must walk before he becomes a man? I answer: there is only one road for man, and it is the road of Jesus Christ, who said, 'I am the way, the truth and the life.'"[36]

CHAPTER 8

THE FORGOTTEN TREE

Virtually every sermon preached today is built on the assumption that you can eventually be a successful Christian if you just try hard enough. "Try harder to be like Christ." "Work at it, and you'll be like Him." "Study your Bible, obey it, and you'll be like Jesus." "Get serious, take Jesus as your model, and you'll be a good disciple." "You become like what you admire. Admire Christ more and you'll be more like Him." So we are told. It's also not uncommon to hear Christian groups and churches say, "We're just trying to be like Jesus." The message is: "Imitate Jesus, and you'll be just like Him."

But as we saw in a previous chapter, this isn't the gospel. Neither can you find such a thought in the New Testament.

Most of the exhortations in sermons and books to "follow Jesus" and "imitate Jesus" are built on a profound flaw. That flaw is this: All you have to do is stick your nose in the Gospels, find out what Jesus did, and then, voilà. Do it yourself. You will then be a good Christian.

Let's consider what people find when they put their noses in the New Testament. Christians from some traditions only nose out healing the sick, casting out devils, and performing miracles, so they try to do those things. Christians from other traditions only sniff out feeding the poor, standing with the oppressed, and loving sinners, so those are the things they try to do. Christians from still other traditions focus on living holy lives and keeping their noses clean, so they wrinkle up their noses at the world, the flesh, and the devil.

But few smell the fragrance of the whole of Jesus' life and ministry.

As we have already argued, every person who has set out to try to be like Jesus has come to one inescapable conclusion (the ones who are honest, at least): trying to be like Jesus is an impossible undertaking. You will fail at it again and again. The reason, however, is rarely discussed.

> No man knows
> how bad he is, 'til
> he has tried very hard
> to be good.
> —C. S Lewis[1]

It's because we look at the *fruit* of what Jesus did but ignore the *root* behind His actions. We are like those who dissect an orange and try to duplicate it in a laboratory, without ever asking the basic questions: "What produced this orange? How did it happen exactly?"

THE SOURCE OF JESUS' LIFE

First off, Jesus said something that every disciple should grasp and never forget. It's startling when you first read it. Nonetheless, it's a basic truth we must understand if we are to make any real progress in the Lord: *Jesus Christ could not be a "successful" Christian, and He admitted it.*

Consider His own words:

Most assuredly, I say to you, the Son can do nothing of Himself . . .[2]

I can of Myself do nothing.[3]

Now behold, one came and said to Him, "Good Teacher, what good thing shall I do that I may have eternal life?" So He said to him, "Why do you call Me good? No one is good but One, that is, God."[4]

Jesus Christ, your Lord, stated very clearly that He could do nothing in His own energy. What is more, He said that only His Father was good.

So how exactly did Jesus live His life while on earth? If He couldn't do anything on His own, how did He live so flawlessly?

Look at His answer:

Whatever the Father does the Son also does.[5]

I judge only as I hear, and my judgment is just, for I seek not to please myself but him who sent me.[6]

I do nothing on my own but speak just what the Father has taught me.[7]

For I did not speak of my own accord, but the Father who sent me commanded me what to say and how to say it.[8]

Don't you believe that I am in the Father, and that the Father is in me? The words I say to you are not just my own. Rather, it is the Father, living in me, who is doing his work.[9]

Jesus did not live by His own natural strength. Instead, He lived by the energy of His Father who indwelled Him.

He spoke when His Father spoke through Him.

He worked when His Father worked through Him.

He made judgments when His Father judged within Him.

Jesus only did what the Father did, and He did it by means of His Father's indwelling life.

Therein lies the root of Jesus' amazing life. Yet few people talk about it today.

THE TORCH GETS PASSED

We know that Jesus lived by His Father's life. But what about us fallen mortals? What about us Christians?

According to the many sermons we hear preached today, one would think that Jesus gave us a completely different way to live than the way He lived. Jesus said clearly that He couldn't do anything in His own strength. But we are told (or it's heavily implied) that *we* can.

The presupposition that sits underneath virtually every sermon heralded today and most of the Christian books that fill the bookstores is that we can live the Christian life if we just try hard enough. If we just study our Bible more, pray more, witness more, tithe more, hear more sermons . . . then we can be like Jesus.

But that's not the gospel.

The gospel teaches that just as Jesus couldn't do anything of Himself, we can't do anything of *our*selves. Listen to the Lord again: "Without *Me* you can do nothing."[10] The "Christian life" is impossible. It's only *Him*-possible. We can try as hard as we wish to be like Christ, but human effort will never touch the hem of that garment. It's like trying to square a circle. It's like paddling into the gale with one oar. It's like building and operating a motel along a highway that never gets built.

The glory of the gospel is that we who are fallen, tarnished, and marred have been invited to live our lives in the exact same way that Jesus lived His life: by an indwelling Lord.

Let's go back to resurrection day. It is evening. Jesus appears to ten fearful men in a sealed room. He penetrates the door and stands before them.

The Lord bids them peace, and then He takes a deep breath. As a resurrected, life-giving Spirit, the Lord Jesus Christ breathes into these men the wind of God's own life.

Behold we show you a mystery: Just as God the Father lived in Jesus, so now God the Son will begin to live in these ten men. The "only begotten" has now become "the firstborn among many brethren," and God is now the Father of these disciples.

Go to My brethren and say to them, "I am ascending to My Father, and your Father, and to My God and your God."[11]

From this point on, the apostles began to live their lives the same way Jesus Christ lived His—by the power of an indwelling Lord. The passage moved from the Father living out His life in the Son, to the Son living out His life in the disciples.

Point: What the Father was to Jesus Christ, Jesus Christ is to you. *He's your indwelling Lord.* When the veil of the temple was ripped from top to bottom, He got out and we got in.

> Jesus cried out again with a loud voice, and yielded up His spirit. Then, behold, the veil of the temple was torn in two from top to bottom; and the earth quaked, and the rocks were split.[12]

> Therefore, brethren, having boldness to enter into the Holiest by the blood of Jesus, by a new and living way which He consecrated for us, through the veil, that is, His flesh.[13]

But there is more. Because all the fullness of the Godhead was pleased to dwell in Christ, the Father and the Spirit also are pleased to dwell in you. As amazing as it sounds, the entire Trinitarian community has taken up residence inside of you.

You, then, are the victim of a divine conspiracy. You have become the habitat of the living God.

Knowing Christ as your "rest" and allowing Him to live His life through you is one of the most freeing things that you can know as a Christian. "He who has entered His rest has himself also ceased from his works as God did from His."[14]

Resting in Christ doesn't mean being passive. It means allowing the Lord to do the heavy lifting. Laziness is no more the way to follow Jesus than is busyness.

He who calls you is faithful, who also will do it.[15]

For it is God who works in you both to will and to do for His good pleasure.[16]

THE CHOICE OF TWO TREES

When the Creator planted the garden of Eden, He put two trees in the center of it. Today, these same trees stand at the center of life.

The meaning of the tree of the knowledge of good and evil can be understood by the serpent's promise: "By eating from this tree, you will be making your *own* decision. You will be like God, determining for *yourself* what is right and what is wrong."

The fall of humanity was all about women and men assuming the posture that they don't need anyone to tell them what to do. They would decide for themselves what's good and what's bad. They would be self-sufficient and self-determining.

Of course, what was ignored in that whole discussion is the tree of life.

God wanted humans to eat from the tree of life. Eating from the tree of life meant receiving the uncreated life of God into oneself. The tree of life was God's own life made accessible to human beings.

Today, the tree of life is the Lord Jesus Christ.

I am the true vine. . . . As the living Father hath sent Me, and I live by the Father: so he that eateth me, even he shall live by me.[17]

As we have already seen, when we receive Christ, we receive the life of God. Divine life becomes ours. Receiving Christ is simply taking the first bite from the right tree.

Living by God's life is very different from living by the tree of the knowledge of good and evil. A person who is living by the tree of life doesn't sit back and say, "Let me try to do good and avoid evil." Instead, he allows the life of God to flow within and through him. He *yields* to the instincts, promptings, and energy of that God-life.

You see, "good" is a form of life. And only God is good.

Here are the two choices before you today:

1. The choice to intellectually *know* good from evil and to *try* to do good = the tree of the knowledge of good and evil.
2. Living by the life of God, which is goodness itself = the tree of life.

Mark it down: the knowledge of good is the accepted counterfeit to living by life.

The Christian religion[18] is built on the tree of the knowledge of good and evil. The Christian religion can be studied using the same categories of thought used to study any other world religion. It can be analyzed just as Islam, Judaism, and Buddhism are analyzed. The difficulty with the Christian religion (like all religions) is that it makes its adherents think that they have now found the real knowledge of good and evil.

Religion gives people the notion that they have God under control. Religion says that we can understand God absolutely and completely. We can predict what the Almighty will do tomorrow. The Christian religion teaches that the Bible answers virtually every question that's brought to the sacred text. The problem with this line of thought is that the true God cannot fit into anyone's box. God will always end up breaking out of our human expectations and understanding. Every attempt to capture God and cram and ram Him in a system will ultimately fail.

The true God is an untamed lion. He cannot be controlled. The true God *is* the controller.

Yet many Christians have turned the Bible into a form of the knowledge of good and evil. They approach the Bible as raw material by which they can gain control over their lives, so life can be more understandable and under control, less unnerving and unpredictable.

> Oh that we discerning
> Its most holy learning,
> Lord, may love and
> fear Thee, Evermore
> be near Thee!
> —Henry Baker's hymn about
> the Bible[19]

This is a profoundly grievous misuse of the Bible.

Jesus didn't misuse the Scriptures to gain control and predictability in His own life. To Him, the Scriptures were simply the joystick on the Father's controller. They were the instrument through which He got to know His Father better and to discover how to live out His mission.

JESUS AND THE PHARISEES

The Pharisees were the self-appointed guardians of the Judaic religion. They were highly concerned about the moral state of Israel. The Pharisees looked around and said, "There are lots of people in this country who have degenerate moral values. In order for us to put a stop to it, we'll have nothing to do with such people. We will not eat at table with them. We will not talk to them. We will ostracize them completely. In this way, we will faithfully uphold the highest possible moral values."

This outlook spilled over to the Jewish chief priests of the first century. The priests even possessed a private bridge linking their homes to the temple so they wouldn't have to mingle with the common people.

The Pharisees' attempt to promote high moral values was based on the knowledge of good and evil. For this reason, the Lord Jesus—who had a bad reputation of being a "friend of sinners"[20]— constantly collided with the leaven-dispensing Pharisees.

Jesus pushed the boundaries of religion to their limits. He was also a fierce critic of the priestly temple system of His day, decrying its wrongs.

If you examine Jesus' exchanges with the Pharisees, you'll discover a common thread. The Pharisees would ask a question on one level, and Jesus would answer it on a completely different level. The contrast was sometimes so stark that it would appear that Jesus was answering a different question.

Why is this? It's because the Pharisees' questions were coming from the tree of the knowledge of good and evil. And Jesus' response was coming from the tree of life—the life of God.

Jesus went to the people who were shunned by the temple priests: the lame, the blind, the infirm, the lepers, the prostitutes, and even the tax collectors—all of whom were notorious outcasts of society. (The common view of that day was that if you were sick, you deserved it.) Jesus quickly became the champion of the poor, the ostracized, the oppressed and dispossessed. He ministered to those who were marginalized by society, those regarded as valueless.[21]

By doing so, the Lord upstaged the temple system, shaking all of its cages. He rattled the Pharisees by overturning their social customs, norms, and structures. He outraged the priests by claiming to speak for God. He broke down many of the barriers that separated people. And in the process, He was put to death by their collapse.

Regrettably, there is a great deal of pharisaism in the Christian family today.

The Bible teaches the highest possible moral values. But the Bible is fundamentally not about morality. Following the Lord Jesus Christ involves living out the highest moral values. But following Jesus is fundamentally not about morality. Conversion to Christ involves a moral transformation of life. But conversion is not fundamentally about morality either. The most moral unsaved person on the planet needs Christ just as much as the most immoral one. It is Christ, not religion, that saves us.

> Miss Maudie stopped rocking, and her voice hardened. "You are too young to understand it," she said, "but sometimes the Bible in the hand of one man is worse than a whiskey bottle in the hand of [another]."
>
> —Harper Lee, *To Kill a Mockingbird* (1960)[22]

Christianity, therefore, is not fundamentally about morality. And it has nothing to do with the tree of knowledge of good and evil.

When we attempt to turn our spirituality into a matter of

morality, we have begun to eat from the wrong tree. The result is the same as what we see with the Pharisees.

AN EXAMPLE OF MODERN PHARISAISM

Case in point: During the 1980s, many Christians retreated to the suburbs and created for themselves a ring of safe suburban churches. Occasionally they would toss out small patches of money to support tiny inner-city missions, but they stayed away from all the people with whom they disapproved. In fact, many of them became preoccupied with promoting movements that were centered around condemning the bad behavior they observed in the culture around them.

These Christians were not mistaken in condemning immoral behavior. But they were profoundly mistaken in their approach to those who were practicing immorality. They were wrong to think that the proper reaction should be to run as fast as they can in the opposite direction lest they become morally polluted.

That is pharisaism, plain and simple. And it's the exact mind-set that your Lord opposed and taught against. Yet this mind-set took over a large segment of the Christian population in the 1980s, and it's still with us today.

There's a fundamental flaw in the agenda that says that Christians must deal with the world by keeping it at arm's length. This agenda fleshes itself out when believers toss condemnations against the world from a distance. It fleshes itself out in the unholy sentiment that leads us to picking up the nearest doctrinal and moral ball bat and hitting the world over the head with it as hard as possible—and feeling justified with such brutality.

Living by the tree of life is the antidote for this.

Those who live by the life of Christ do not act as though they are morally superior to others. While they stand separate from the defilements of sin and the world, they embrace those who are wounded, hurt, confused, and defiled by them. So on the one hand, believers are "set apart from sinners," but on the other hand, they are the *friends* of sinners.

> Such a high priest meets our need—one who is holy, blameless, pure, set apart from sinners. . . . The Son of Man came eating and drinking, and they say, "Look, a glutton and a winebibber, a friend of tax collectors and sinners!" But wisdom is justified by her [actions].[23]

It was Christ's compassion for the brokenhearted and rejected that drew women and men to Him. And He is the same today as He was then.

Herein lies the missing keynote in the church's approach to the world. If our faith is based on partaking of the wrong tree, we will act like modern Pharisees. If we partake of the tree of life, we will be empowered to go into a godless world as servants of its unacknowledged Lord.

It is critical for us, then, to learn that the life of Christ is within us. And by following that life and yielding to it, we can display the same Jesus who shook the world, conquered sin and death, set the captives free, and lives forevermore.

Right now, countless nonbelievers view Christians as hypocritical, judgmental, irrelevant, boring, and self-righteous. This is because so many Christians have never learned what it means to eat from the tree of life. Instead, they have been given a steady diet of the tree of the knowledge of good and evil.

To be perfectly candid, there are few things that are as dull and boring in life as Christianity without the living, breathing, radiant, triumphant Christ. It's a first-degree snoozer. If you could bottle it, you would have the cure for insomnia.

But there is nothing in life that is more fascinating than Christ. He is the most exciting person in the universe, bar none. But we are speaking about the real Christ, not the shallow, anemic, insipid "Jesus" that's so often promoted today.

Consequently, when God's people begin living by an indwelling Lord, the world begins to get a glimpse of the real Jesus. The result? All of their negative experiences about religion, Christianity, and moral condemnation are overcome by the steady, regular, persistent, and stubborn extension of God's imponderable love in Christ for them.

> We cannot live the Christian life on our own or by our own strength, and Jesus says, "I never said you could. I always said I would."
>
> —Dr. Terrence Kelshaw, bishop, diocese of the Rio Grande[24]

When you enter into a dark place, it's better to light a candle than curse the darkness.

So this is the Lord's challenge for our day: to move beyond the religious knowledge of good and evil and into a full *yieldedness* to the life of Christ that beats within every child of God. Human energy in the work of God won't cut it. It's one thing to work *for* God. It is another to work *with* God. And it's yet another to have God work *through* you. The work of God is God Himself at work.

But the latter only happens when we are living by the tree of life and Christ becomes the motivation *and* the source of our service. In this way, we discover what it means to serve in the Lord's energy rather than our own.

A PEOPLE OF THE PERSON

Sometimes Christians are described as "a people of the book," meaning the Bible. But to be true to the book means being occupied with the person—Jesus Christ. We have a high view of Scripture because we have a high view of Christ, and the two can never be separated.

On the last day of His earthly life, Jesus stood before a Roman provincial governor, Pontius Pilate, and was questioned. "I came into the world to testify to the truth," Jesus said.

Pilate asked Him, "What is truth?"

Jesus didn't answer the question because Pilate was staring at truth and didn't recognize it. Truth is not a book, or a denomination, or a creed, or a liturgy. Truth is a person. And Jesus is His name.

Christianity, therefore, is not fundamentally about following a book. It's about following a person and living out of His life. The library of divinely inspired books we call the Holy Bible best helps us to follow that person, for they testify of Him.

The Bible does not offer a plan or a blueprint for living. The "good news" was not a new list of laws, or an improved set of ethical injunctions, or an amended plan with the latest addenda and corrigenda. The good news was the story of a person's life, as reflected in the Apostles' Creed, where the mystery of faith proclaims this narrative: "Christ has died, Christ has risen, Christ will come again."

The written Word is a map that leads us to the living Word. Or as Jesus Himself put it, "The Scriptures point to Me!"[25] Every part of the sacred text breathes the same oxygen—Christ. So the Bible is not the destination; it's a compass that points to Jesus—heaven's Lodestar.

LOST FOR WORDS

It is all too possible to confuse an academic knowledge or theology about Jesus with a personal knowledge of the living Christ Himself. These two stand as far apart as do the hundred thousand million galaxies.

The Christian faith claims to be rational, but also to reach out to touch ultimate mysteries. So the fullness of Christ can never be accessed through the frontal lobe alone. That's why Jesus did not leave His disciples with CliffsNotes for a systematic theology. He left them with breath and body. He didn't leave them with a coherent and clear belief system by which to love God and others. He gave them wounds to touch and hands to heal. He didn't leave them with intellectual belief or a "Christian worldview." He left them with a relational faith and an indwelling presence.

> Beware you be not swallowed up in books: an ounce of love is worth a pound of knowledge.
> —John Wesley[26]

The Bible does not hit just one note for sixty-six books. It speaks anew to every age. It should be read in the light of new information and fresh discoveries. It must also be understood in community, not as an individual. Both Testaments were written to communities and can only be rightly understood within that same context.[27]

And as one would expect of a Trinitarian faith, participation is required because the reader plays an important role in discovering what the Bible teaches based on the diversities of what we bring to it.

The Bible is not reader-indifferent or history-independent. Each age draws new insights from the Scriptures based on what that age brings to it. This means that revelation is always veiled in mystery. We bring to it our culture, our history, our gaze, and our glasses. The fundamentalist idea that the text has only one meaning is of relatively recent invention (it was spawned from Enlightenment rationalism).[28]

But regardless of your interpretation of Scripture, unless the cutting edge of your life and ministry is Jesus Christ, you're building castles in the sand and skating on invisible ice. That's why, once and for all, the church must be awakened to the Christ who lives within her and begin to understand the limitless resources of His indwelling life.

Or to put it another way, we must begin living by the forgotten tree rather than the forbidden one.[29]

CHAPTER 9

A HOUSE OF FIGS

Jesus Christ cannot be separated from His church. While Jesus is distinct from His Bride, He is not separate from her. She is, in fact, His very own body in the earth.

God has chosen to vest all of power, authority, and life in the living Christ. However, God in Christ is only known fully in and through His church. As Paul said, the manifold wisdom of God—which is Christ—is known through the *ekklesia*.

... to the intent that now the manifold wisdom of God might be made known by the church to the principalities and powers in the heavenly places ...[1]

... Christ the power of God and the wisdom of God.[2]

The authentic Christian life, therefore, is not an individual pursuit. It's a corporate journey. For all today's talk of "community," what matters in life is still primarily played out in a "Youniverse" of inward, self-certifying scrutiny and the privacy of subjective illumination, not dimensions of biblical tradition and community.

But knowing Christ and making Him known is not an individual prospect. Those who insist on flying life solo will be brought to earth with a crash. Thus Christ and His church are intimately joined and connected. And what God has joined together, let no one put asunder. Jesus said, "I am in you and you are in Me, as the Father is in you and you are in Him. You are My sister and you are My brother."[3] This is not some metaphor.

DISCOVERING AND DISPLAYING

You will never know the depths of Christ on your own. It matters not how intelligent, gifted, or spiritual you may be. It takes a functioning body to know Him fully. And it takes a functioning body to display His fullness. Paul made clear in Ephesians that we come to know the width, length, depth, and height of Christ "with all the saints." It's only by being vitally and organically connected with other members of the body in a living way that we experience the fullness of God.

> . . . [that you] may be able to comprehend with all the saints what is the width and length and depth and height—to know the love of Christ which passes knowledge; that you may be filled with all the fullness of God.[4]

In 1 Corinthians 12:1–3, Paul wrote that Jesus Christ is not a mute idol. He has the power of speech. Paul then began to unveil *how* Christ speaks. He speaks through His body (vv. 4–31).

In the midst of this discourse, Paul made this riveting statement: "For as the body is one and has many members, but all the members of that one body, being many, are one body, so also is Christ."[5]

Notice that he didn't say, "so also is the church." He instead said, "so also is Christ." The meaning is striking but clear. *The church is Jesus Christ in corporate expression.* So, properly conceived, the church is the reassembling of Christ so that He might be made visible on the earth.

Dietrich Bonhoeffer said it well when he stated that the church is "Christ existing as community."[6] You cannot separate the head from the body. You cannot separate the vine from the branches. You cannot separate the foundation from the temple. And you cannot separate the Bridegroom from the bride.

Paul's statement in 1 Corinthians 12:12 is a throwback to his initial revelation of Jesus. Recall that when the Lord appeared to Paul in a vision on the Damascus road, he saw and heard "the head" speaking from heaven. But Jesus' words to Paul demonstrated that He and His body were one. "Saul, Saul why are you persecuting *Me*?"[7] To touch the body is to touch Christ, for they are inseparable.

Practically, this means that we know Jesus Christ through one another, not just by ourselves. We see Him, hear Him, touch Him, taste and smell Him through our sisters and brothers within whom He dwells.

Genuine church life is born when groups of people are intoxicated with a glorious unveiling of their Lord. Jesus Christ is the only foundation upon which an authentic church can be built.

Anything else is wood, hay, and stubble.[8] Any work that comes out of Christ is immortal. It will never turn to ash even though fire may fall on it.

> Preaching without spiritual aroma is like a rose without fragrance. We can only get the perfume by getting more of Christ.
>
> —A. B. Simpson[9]

The calling of every person involved in church planting, then, is to build the *ekklesia* upon a ground-breaking revelation of the Son of God—a revelation that burns in the fiber of their being and leaves God's people overwhelmed, bowled over, reeling, and awash with the glories of Christ.

May God give us more people who have had a head-on collision with Jesus, who have caught a glimpse of His radiance, and who, as a result, can meld a group of people together with a living knowledge of their God in the face of Jesus Christ. May He raise up countless servants who can faithfully steward the divine mystery and turn it loose on this world.

ΑΩ

The occupation of every local assembly can be summed up in two words: *discovering* and *displaying*—that is, discovering and displaying Christ. This is the church's chief calling in this world—to manifest the mystery.[10] The church is the tangible manifestation of Christ's life in the world today. Because the church is part of Christ, a revelation of Jesus will eventually lead to a revelation of His church.[11]

THE SIGNIFICANCE OF BETHANY

When Christ entered this world, He was rejected in all quarters. Consider His birth. The entire town of Bethlehem closed its doors to Him. So He was born in a stable amid the stain and stench of cow dung.

When He was about two years old, He was hunted by the government. It wished to kill Him as it had all other boys who were born when He was. (There were no boys in His kindergarten class.)

When He began His ministry around the age of thirty, He was rejected by His own people—the Jews.[12] The religious leaders who dominated Jerusalem also rejected Him. Remember how He wept over the city because they refused to receive their Messiah.[13]

When He sought entrance into Samaria, the city rejected Him.[14] He was also rejected by His own hometown, Nazareth. Remember His words—"A prophet is not without honor except in his own country."[15] Not even His own kin believed in Him.[16]

In short, the Lord had no home on this earth. "Foxes have holes and birds of the air have nests," He said, "but the Son of Man has nowhere to lay His head."[17]

Here is the Creator of the universe—the One who not only made all things but for whom all things were made—and He is rejected. He is neither welcomed nor received.

There was only one exception.

Throughout His entire earthly life, there was only one place on the planet where Jesus Christ was received with welcome. It was a tiny, obscure village called Bethany, just two miles east of Jerusalem, and the home of Mary, Martha, Lazarus, and Simon the leper—Jesus' friends.[18]

Interestingly, on the six days preceding His crucifixion, Jesus went to the city of Jerusalem in the daytime, but He always retreated to Bethany to spend the night. In Bethany, He found refuge, rest, love, and peace.[19]

From Genesis to Revelation, the forces of evil have disputed God's right to have a home on this earth. But from the beginning, God has wanted a "house"—a place where He could rest and "presence" Himself.[20] This is what Bethany symbolizes—a home for Christ.

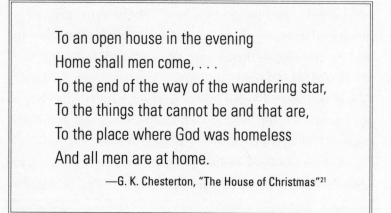

To an open house in the evening
Home shall men come, . . .
To the end of the way of the wandering star,
To the things that cannot be and that are,
To the place where God was homeless
And all men are at home.

—G. K. Chesterton, "The House of Christmas"[21]

Following are some of the outstanding features of Bethany, all of which depict what the Lord is looking for in every city across this planet.

Bethany is the place where Jesus was utterly welcome.

Martha welcomed Him into her house.

—LUKE 10:38

In contrast to everywhere else He went, Jesus was completely and gladly received in Bethany.

What does it mean to receive and welcome the Lord Jesus? It means giving Him the place of primacy. Jesus will not share space with anyone or anything else in that position. He is not at home in any church that doesn't give Him the place of absolute supremacy and sovereignty. Jesus desires to be more than a guest. And His Father expects Him to be Master of the house.

Receiving Christ also means receiving His entire ministry. Some churches receive the Lord's preaching or teaching ministry, but they reject His healing ministry. Some welcome the power of His resurrection, but they reject the fellowship of His sufferings. Some accept His ministry of caring for the poor and oppressed, but they reject His ministry of reaching the lost with the gospel, edifying the believers, and bringing His body into fullness.

To receive Christ in a piecemeal fashion is to receive Him on *our own* terms. We have to receive Him on His terms.

Receiving Christ also means receiving all who belong to Him. On several occasions, Jesus made it clear that in receiving those He loves, we are receiving Him. Those who reject His loved ones are, in fact, rejecting Him.[22]

So, any church that welcomes some members of the body but rejects others is not fully receiving Christ. And any church that welcomes some whom the Lord has sent to His work, while rejecting others, is rejecting Christ.

The outstanding mark of Bethany is that it receives all whom Christ has received. To do otherwise is to say, "Lord, we'll take Your hand and Your arm, but we don't want Your foot or Your leg." To be exclusive and sectarian not only dishonors Him; it also dismembers Him.[23]

The Lord is looking for a place where He is completely received and fully welcomed. Not Christ *plus* something else. Not Christ *minus* a part. But Christ—head and body.

Bethany is the place where women and men are His disciples.

[Martha] had a sister called Mary, who also sat at Jesus' feet and heard His word.

—LUKE 10:39

In this scene, Mary is seated in the living space with the twelve disciples, while Martha is in the kitchen preparing a meal. But Mary is crossing an invisible line. She is breaching two social boundaries.

First, she is sitting in the men's space (the living room in that day). Second, she is sitting in the posture of a disciple. Every first-century rabbi had male disciples only. Jesus was the exception. He was the only teacher in antiquity to include women in His circle of followers.

Martha protests to Jesus, but the Lord's response to her is tender. "Martha, Martha, you are troubled about many things," He tells her, "but only one thing is necessary, and Mary has chosen it. I won't take it away from her."

What do you suppose Jesus was talking about here? The one thing that is necessary—"that good part," as Jesus called it in Luke 10:42—is to love Christ. And out of that love, friendship, and fellowship will automatically flow intelligent service.

Many Christians today are busy serving God, doing many things for Him in many diverse places (church kitchens, soup kitchens, boardrooms, sacred buildings, mission trips, convention centers, etc.). Some burn out and break down because of it. But how many know the secret of loving Christ, sitting at His feet, listening to Him share His heart, and allowing His life to be the source of their service?

The greatest priority in life is to know the Lord. Upon knowing Him, we will be drawn to love and serve Him. Bethany is the place where both women and men sit at His feet and hear His word.

> Our faith is not primarily the assent to facts about God but friendship with God. This man Jesus offers us more than words about God, spiritual insight. He did not come to promote values. He did not come to tell us about God's friendship for us. He is God's friendship with us made flesh and blood.
> —Timothy Radcliffe[24]

Bethany is the place where Christ is loved and befriended.

The sisters sent to Him, saying, "Lord, behold, he whom You love is sick." . . . *[Jesus said to His disciples,] "Our friend Lazarus sleeps, but I go that I may wake him up."*

—JOHN 11:3, 11

Bethany is the place where Jesus Christ loves His own, and they know it. It's also the place of friendship—friendship with the living God.

Jesus desires friends over servants. He desires love over servitude.

Some of His last words to His disciples (last words are usually important) were "No longer do I call you servants, for a servant does not know what his master is doing; but I have called you friends, for all things that I heard from My Father I have made known to you."[25]

It is possible to serve without loving. But Jesus Christ is the greatest Lover in the universe. And it is love and friendship that He desires and delights in most.[26] In the cold temple of Jerusalem, God was served. But in the warmth of a Bethany home, He was loved and befriended.

Bethany is the place of death and resurrection.

Jesus called in a loud voice, "Lazarus, come out!" The dead man came out.

—John 11:43–44 NIV

In this gripping scene, Lazarus has died. Grief and confusion surround Jesus. Mourning and sorrow thicken the air. God's greatest mortal enemy—death—has taken one whom Jesus loves.

The Lord is deeply disturbed. Even though He knows He's going to liberate Lazarus from the chains of death, He is still touched by the sorrow that has afflicted His beloved friends and the whole village.

It's a heart-stopping moment. The One who created the universe is weeping at the grave of His friend. But He who is the Resurrection and the Life raises him from the dead.

In resurrection, God starts all over again with a new creation. But resurrection always follows suffering and death.

So there is crisis and suffering in Bethany. There is death also.

The cross sits at the very center of a body of believers that authentically gathers as the church. They will experience death—dry spells; sufferings with one another; death to their agendas, aspirations, opinions, and preferences; and crisis. But this is how God builds His house. Out of the dying, the Lord's life is expressed, and we are built together into a home for Jesus Christ. From the mulch of decay, disease, and death, God births His resurrection life.[27]

> God's clock keeps perfect time.
> —Mabel Boggs Sweet

Note that Jesus waited four days after Lazarus' death before He raised him up. Death is hopeless. But four days after death is *beyond* hopeless.

But never forget: every crisis you face is a God-given opportunity to rediscover Christ in a bold new way. For that reason, every painful encounter we meet bears the fingerprints of God.

When Paul was suffering, Jesus told him, "My grace is sufficient."[28] The Lord's grace, however, sometimes comes long after the insufficiency. So be prepared to meet a God who seems to have the disturbing habit of leaving the scene when you most need Him. This includes times when you are courting death and your life is hanging in the balance.

But remember this—especially when you're tempted to go into light panic mode. He *is* resurrection and He *is* life. And if you endure, outwaiting your impatience for His timing, Christ will roll the stone away and raise you from the dead. While you may stumble and fumble at the goal line, Jesus will eventually carry you across.

Bethany is the place of liberty from bondage.

The dead man came out, his hands and feet wrapped with strips of linen, and a cloth around his face. Jesus said to them, "Take off the grave clothes and let him go."

—John 11:44 NIV

Consider the Lord's command: "Take off the grave clothes and let him go." Now look at Lazarus in the tomb. His body is beginning to decay, so much so that it stinks, and he is bound with the robes of death.

Yet by His word—"Lazarus, come out!"—Jesus dispenses His resurrection life, and Lazarus is made alive. And then Jesus utters these words: "Take off the grave clothes and let him go!"

This was a command to the crowd. Jesus did not unbind Lazarus. *He told the crowd to do it.*

We discover two things here: First, Bethany is the place where God's people are set free from all bondages: bondage to religion, to legalism, to sin, to the world, to serving God in the flesh, and every other kind of bondage.

If we know anything about Jesus Christ at all, we know this: He's the most liberated person in the universe. And He liberates all who turn to Him in faith.

Second, we are the Lord's colleagues in setting others free. God will not do for us what we can do for ourselves. It was as if the Lord were saying, "I freed him from the powers of death. Now *you* free him from the clothes of death. I want you to co-labor with Me in bringing freedom to others. Since I have set you free, you are now My agents to set others free." Such is the nature of resurrection life.

"Loose him and let him go," is the word that the Lord gives to all who live in Bethany.

Bethany is the place where the supreme worth of Christ is recognized.

Then Mary took about a pint of pure nard, an expensive perfume; she poured it on Jesus' feet and wiped his feet with her hair. And the house was filled with the fragrance of the perfume.

—JOHN 12:3 NIV

Here we have an inimitable picture of what Bethany is all about. A feast is given in honor of Jesus. The Lord is seated at the head of the table—the place of honor and supremacy. There is feasting, fellowship, and unbounded joy.

This same story as recorded in Matthew 26 and Mark 14 gives more details: The feast is at the home of Simon the leper, whom Jesus may have healed in the past, because, in this scene, he's a cleansed leper. Yet even though Simon no longer has leprosy, he still carries a stigma. People still fear him. They still ostracize him.

But not Jesus.[29]

Also present is Lazarus—a friend who has been raised from the dead. Cleansed lepers and resurrected friends all sitting around a table where Christ is head—eating, laughing, telling stories, playing. *This is a family feasting in the presence of Jesus Christ.* They are supping with Him, and He with them. That's Bethany. It's a riveting picture of authentic church life.

Jesus' body is laid out twice in the Bible: once on a table, and once in a tomb.[30] The body on the supper table is eaten not with family but with friends. But these friends became Jesus' new family, and they would soon become His new body.

Mary has with her a sealed flask of precious perfume. It's nard from India. Extremely expensive. She breaks open the seal and pours the perfume upon the Lord's head as though He were a king. As the perfume trickles down His body and reaches His feet, she anoints them with the perfume.

Jesus interprets the act as preparation for His burial. Mary is anointing Him as one would a corpse—a royal one.[31]

The perfume is worth three hundred denarii. A denarius is a day's wage. Three hundred denarii, therefore, is nearly a year's salary. At the time of this writing, the average annual income in America is $46,000. So the value of Mary's flask of perfume was about equivalent to $46,000 USD. You won't find this fragrance at the mall. This is the most expensive perfume in the world.

This was probably Mary's family inheritance. It represented her savings, her future, her security. Therefore, Mary's act demonstrates extravagant worship. Profuse loyalty. Larger-than-life beauty. Lavish love and devotion. It recalls the words of Paul from prison: "I consider everything a loss compared to the surpassing greatness of knowing Christ Jesus my Lord, for whose sake I have lost all things. I consider them rubbish, that I may gain Christ."[32]

In Bethany, Jesus Christ is valued for His exceeding worth. There is nothing too costly to lay at His feet.

When the flask was broken, the house surrendered to the aroma of the perfume. Herein lies a great truth: *When the vessel is broken, the fragrance of Christ pours forth.*

When a people allow themselves to be broken by their

Lord—when they are willing to "waste" themselves upon Christ—
the fragrance of His life can be sensed by those who come near.

> Thanks be to God, who always leads us in triumphal procession
> in Christ and through us spreads everywhere the fragrance of
> the knowledge of Him.[33]

> The house was filled with the fragrance.[34]

But listen to Judas's reaction—and according to the other
accounts of this story, the other disciples reacted the same way.
What did they say? Three words: *Why this waste?*

"Why this waste?" they protested. "You could have helped the
poor with this small fortune."[35] The disciples were scandalized
that Jesus had defended luxury over justice.

Mary's dazzling act of devotion exposed their hearts.

Few things are as close to God's heart as helping the poor
and the oppressed. But *preeminently* important is Jesus Christ
Himself. He is more significant than any ministry, no matter how
good or noble. It is possible to worship the god of "ministry" in
place of Christ. In fact, we can "goddify" almost anything—even
good things like family, justice, helping the poor, health and nutri-
tion, Christian fellowship, service, etc. But only Christ is central.
Everything else is only to Him and for Him.

To waste means to give more than is necessary. The message
here is that it is impossible to give more than is necessary to Jesus.
If our eyes are open to see His infinite value, we will "waste" our
lives on Him gladly and even recklessly, just as Mary did.

Bethany is the place where Christ is ministered to.

Jesus entered Jerusalem and went to the temple. He looked around at everything, but since it was already late, he went out to Bethany with the Twelve.

—MARK 11:11 NIV

On Sunday morning, Jesus entered the city of Jerusalem, riding on a colt. He entered the holy city as a humble King.[36] Before sundown the same day, He left Jerusalem and returned to Bethany, where He lodged.[37] On Monday morning, He headed to Jerusalem again. On the way there, He hungered and saw a fig tree with leaves. But upon closer examination, He discovered that it lacked figs.[38]

This was a strange situation. When a fig tree puts forth leaves, it's shouting that it has figs. But not this tree. It was deceptive and defective. It was announcing that it possessed fruit, but it really had none at all.

The fig tree could not feed the hungry, including our hungry Lord. It could not satisfy His heart or His belly.

Hoarding the fruit for itself, the tree didn't produce any figs. So Jesus cursed it, and it withered away. This is a stark omen of what failing to reproduce and bear fruit for others can lead to. The church that keeps alive the image of Christ can be the same church that betrays that image and stomps it into the ground by hoarding its fruit for its own purposes.

But there was a place that could feed the Lord. There was a place that could satisfy His heart.

At sundown, Jesus returned to Bethany.[39] There our Lord was fed. He was cared for. He was loved. And He was satisfied.

Strikingly, Bethany means "house of figs."[40]

According to many scholars, the fig tree represents Judaism—the religious establishment of Jesus' people. Israel was supposed to feed our Lord, but she did not. Instead, the nation rejected Him. "He came to His own, and His own did not receive Him."[41]

But thank God, there was a place that could feed Him. There was a people—a faithful remnant—who could give Him rest and satisfaction. That people and place was Bethany—the house full of figs.

A prophet may be without honor in his own country, but Jesus Christ found a home in Bethany.

Bethany is the place of ascension.

He led them out as far as Bethany, and He lifted up His hands and blessed them. Now it came to pass, while He blessed them, that He was parted from them and carried up into heaven.

—LUKE 24:50–52

As we have seen, a death and a resurrection occurred in Bethany. But there was also an ascension.

After His resurrection, Jesus Christ ascended into the heavenly realm. And from where did He ascend? *He ascended from Bethany.*

When Christ ascended, He was enthroned as absolute head over all things. And all things were placed under His feet.[42] Paul tells us that we, too, ascended with Christ and are now seated with Him in heavenly places.[43]

Christians aren't saved from all troubles or delivered from all problems. But we have been given an ascendant life with which to rise above them. If you take your place *in Christ* in heavenly places, you will discover the meaning of ascension. Only Jesus Christ can transfix and then transfigure the void at the heart of the church.

We are seated in "heavenly places in Christ," and since all things are under His feet, all things are under ours as well. This doesn't mean that the world is our footstool or our football. But it does mean that we can walk with Jesus without feeling as if we have one foot on a banana peel and the other foot in a grave. It means that we can leave the footprint of our Lord wherever we go.

It is our task to remind one another of this reality and believe it together, because walking in this truth means receiving the power of the Spirit for life and ministry. When Christ ascended and was glorified, the Spirit was poured out.[44] In other words, He descended in the Spirit,[45] and we became His new body.

> Then Christ will make his home in your hearts.
> —Ephesians 3:17 NLT

But there is something else. Jesus' ascension and enthronement proved that He is the "head over all things to the church."[46] It is our responsibility to submit to His headship and express it in the earth.

In Bethany, Jesus Christ is given His rightful place as absolute, exclusive head. He is not simply a welcomed guest. He is the Master of the house. And that house is not just a lodging for Him; it becomes His home.

THE EARTH'S LONGING

The earth awaits a body of Christians in every city who will receive Jesus utterly and completely.

A body who will esteem Him above everything else, giving Him His rightful place of supremacy.

A body who will give themselves utterly to Christ and to one another.

A body who will be more family than bless-me club, and who will never stop hearing the ringing of truth: "For better or for worse, I will never leave you nor forsake you . . . and not even death will part us."

A body who is willing to "waste" their lives on Him together and dig their feet in the ground and say, "This place is for Christ. We claim Him as absolute Lord here. Let all hell rage against it. We are here by Him, through Him, and for Him—come hell or Hiawatha."

A body who will stand for God's supreme interest in the earth—a dwelling place for His fullness—a spiritual Bethany.

A body who will participate inside Jesus' own relationship with His Father, and, in so doing, discover that our true home is found in the love of the Father, Son, and Holy Spirit.

A body where Jesus has so taken their breath away that they can no longer breathe on their own, but by the Holy Spirit—the breath of the living God.

The earth eagerly awaits such.

May it come. And may our Lord have what His soul longs for—a Bethany in every town—a place where He can lay His head and breathe His breath.

Is He not worthy of such a place today?

CHAPTER 10

WHO IS THIS LORD OF YOURS?

Christians have always held to the eternal mystery that God is triune: Father, Son, and Spirit—one God, three persons, one substance.[1]

That said, our exaltation of the Lord Jesus in no way diminishes the Father or the Spirit or robs them of their glory. The question of the Trinity takes us beyond the scope of this book, but elsewhere we have discussed how the Trinitarian community is the basis for the church and how the shape of the church is rooted in the fellowship of the Godhead.[2]

From the beginning, God eternally poured all of Himself into His Son by the Spirit, and the Son eternally poured Himself into His Father by the Spirit. Immanuel Kant could not have been more wrong when he wrote dismissively of the Trinity in the eighteenth century, "The Trinity has got no relevance to practical living."[3] The eternal dance of divine life, love, communion, participation, and self-emptying within the triune God is central to the Christian life, to ministry, to the community of faith and the faithfulness of its mission.[4] Most of all, it teaches us that just as God is not alone even when God is alone, so you are not alone even when you are alone. We don't have to go down to the "valley of the shadow" all alone.

> If you see charity, you see the Trinity. For you see the one who loves, the one loved, and the love that unites them.
> —St. Augustine[5]

It is only through Jesus Christ that we enter into this eternal dance. And it is only through Christ that we come to know the triune God and the loving fellowship of the Father, Son, and Spirit.[6] As John tells us, the incarnate Son is the Father's self-utterance and self-expression.[7] As Paul tells us, the fullness of the Godhead dwells in Christ.[8] All the fullness, the sum total, the full supply and reservoir of Godhood is concentrated in Jesus.

For this reason Dietrich Bonhoeffer, who conceived of his life as a "witness to Jesus Christ," said, "In Jesus Christ the reality of God entered into the reality of this world. . . . Henceforward one can speak neither of God nor of the world without speaking of Jesus Christ. All concepts of reality which do not take account of him are abstractions."[9]

A FALSE DICHOTOMY

There is a disturbing trend today. Many Christians have separated the Jesus of history from the Christ of faith. Those who promote this disconnect fall off one side of the horse or the other. They either focus on the Jesus of the Gospels to the neglect of the Christ that Paul presented in his letters, or they focus on Paul's revelation of Christ (usually as Savior in both Romans and Galatians) and make the Jesus of the Gospels an endnote.

Neither view lands us in the saddle. Both make the fundamental flaw of turning the Jesus of the Gospels into someone different from the Jesus revealed in Paul's letters.

But the truth is that the Jesus who walked the shores of Galilee is the same person who indwells the church today. There is no disconnect between the Jesus of Mark's Gospel and the incredible, all-sufficient, cosmic Christ of Colossians. The Christ who lived in the first century had a preexistence before time, and a postexistence, after time as we know it has ended. He is Alpha *and* Omega, Beginning *and* End, A *and* Z all at the same moment. He stands in the future and at the end of the age at the same second that He exists within every child of God. Failure to embrace these paradoxical truths has created monumental problems and generated divisive debates (open versus classical theism, election versus free will, and so on) and has diminished Christ's greatness in the eyes of God's people.

For those who are inclined to pit the Jesus of the Gospels against the Christ of the epistles, let's look at our Lord's earthly life in light of "the mystery" (see chapter 2).

LOOKING UNTO JESUS

Let's go back to the first century and take another look at our Lord. "Come and behold Him." We bless and are blessed as we simply "behold Him," not as we boast of talents or do great things, but as "we look full in His wonderful face."[10] Everyday "beholding" releases Jesus, especially when that beholding is done by a community.

Watch Him at a wedding in Cana. According to the custom of that day, the bridegroom was responsible for supplying the food and wine. You know the story. The wine ran out. This represented a social disgrace—a grave oversight on the part of the bridegroom.

Behold your Lord's first miracle. He turns water into wine—but no ordinary wine. He creates a wine that is finer than the wine that had run out. In one brilliant stroke of compassion, Jesus Christ removes the bridegroom's shame. He supplies the lack. He covers the mistake. He removes the disgrace. He reverses the failure. And He makes the bridegroom look like a champion.

What a Christ.

Watch Him as He encounters a battered, abused, shamed, and forgotten woman. She's a Samaritan of ill repute—a five-time divorcée. Your Lord breaks all social conventions by talking to her in public. But that's not all. He shares with her one of the greatest truths that a human being can know. In addition, He breaks Jewish custom by using her utensils and eating with her friends in a Samaritan village (something Jews were forbidden to do). Here is a Lord who embraces a dejected woman and woos her and her friends to Himself.

What a Christ.

Watch Him as He allows a prostitute to love Him in the house of a Pharisee. She pours expensive perfume on His feet, unbinds her hair and uses it as a towel to anoint His feet. Such an act is scandalous (for a woman to unbind her hair in that day was akin to publically removing her bra in our day). The Pharisees move into high-octane-judgment mode toward Jesus and the woman.

And what does the Lord do? He accepts this woman's extravagant act of love and adoration and rebukes the finger-pointing Pharisee for his self-righteousness, saying, "Her sins, which are many, are forgiven, for she loved much. But to whom little is forgiven, the same loves little." To the woman He said, "Your faith has saved you. Go in peace."[11]

What a Christ.

Watch Him as He sits before a woman caught in the act of adultery. See her with bleeding cuts on her body, dragged like a rag doll before a hungry mob of judgmental men, waiting for the first stone to crush her head and bring her to a death that she justly deserves. Behold your glorious Lord. He asks one question, a question that pierces the heart of every man who is ready to send this woman to her grave. Mesmerized by the Lord's words, each man drops his stone and walks away. Christ's parting words to the guilty woman? "Neither do I condemn you; go and sin no more."[12]

What a Christ!

As we read the Gospel accounts, we cannot help but be awestruck by the wonderful person they present. Yet the startling reality is that this *same* Radiance that we marvel at in the pages of our New Testaments has come to continue His life in and through us.

Genuine Christianity is learning to live by an indwelling Christ. Consequently, the Christian life should be reframed as God's life come to earth and displayed visibly through human beings. The Christian life is the outflow of "Christ in you," the breaking forth of God's uncreated, indwelling life—the radiating of God's own energy in fallen, human vessels.

But we have this treasure in earthen vessels, that the excellence of the power may be of God and not of us.[13]

Seeing Christianity from this perspective changes everything.

Turn your eyes upon Jesus,
Look full in His wonderful face,
And the things of earth will grow strangely dim,
In the light of His glory and grace.

—Helen H. Lemmel.[14]

IT'S HIS TIME

We live in a day when what sells best in the Christian world are books, sermons, and television programs that are aimed directly at *you*—*This Is* Your *Day*, You *Are the Reason for the Season*, *Become a Better* You, *It's* Your *Time*, *The* Me *I Want to Be*, *The Life* You've *Always Wanted*, and similar titles orbiting around the Youniverse. We would now like to take all the arrows that point to *you* and bend them back to our Lord.

Behold the ill-starred Nazarene who went about "doing good and healing all who were oppressed by the devil."[15]

Behold the artisan from Galilee, the one who called Himself the "Son of Man" (which means "son of Adam"—"the human being").

Watch Him as He is taken before Rome's delegates in the city of Jerusalem. See Him standing before Pilate—rejected, dejected, bludgeoned, beaten, spat upon. Behold Him who created the heavens, the Lord of the universe, suffering the most horrific, gruesome form of torture that was ever invented by the human imagination.

Observe Him hanging on a wooden stake, dying a slow, hideous death, covered with blood—naked, mocked, and shamed. The Messiah has become a public spectacle that elicits the spine-chilling, gleeful laughter of satan himself.

Watch death, the child of sin, emerge from the pit. With open arms, it darkens the wood of the cross and takes the Prince of heaven into its silent, hopeless domain.

ΑΩ

The powers of Rome may have defeated the suffering artisan two thousand years ago, but in the end, He shall triumph. Christ shall subdue all things and put them under His feet, for upon that bloody hill, Jesus of Nazareth—the spotless, sinless man— defeated the powers of darkness and won for Himself the keys of death, hell, and the grave. He is a Savior to the uttermost for our "guttermost." He saves in every situation and at all times. There is no circumstance too hard for Him.

By Jesus' resurrection, God the Father vindicated Him before angels, demons, and the human race to be the universally triumphant, sovereign Lord. This same Jesus now sits at the right hand of power, as a faithful high priest, tirelessly interceding for His own in the presence of God. He lives by the power of an endless life, and He never fails.

> The one foundation, the unshakable support of the universe is Christ, who upholds all things, and preserves in well-being all that has been firmly founded. We are all built upon him: we are a spiritual house bonded together by the Spirit to form a holy temple which is his own dwelling place, for he dwells in our hearts through faith.
>
> —St. Cyril of Alexandria[16]

And one day, every kingdom, every ruler, every principality and power shall bow their mortal knees to the rejected Nazarene. He, the Lamb of God,[17] the Lion of the tribe of Judah,[18] shall reign in regal glory over everything in, below, and above the earth, in heaven.[19] He shall be the judge of all creation, and His kingdom shall never end.[20]

In that day, Jesus the Nazarene shall be universally vindicated as the ruler of the kings of the earth. Humanity will meet the power of glory face-to-face, for when He appears, the world will see His divinity, His beauty, His majestic splendor, His perfect righteousness, and His complete holiness. He shall make all crooked lines straight as the earth's rightful judge.[21] But more, all who follow Him today will share in the unveiled, unapproachable, indescribable radiance of God's Son tomorrow—a greater glory than this world could ever comprehend.[22]

Indeed, it will be *His* time, and He will have the last word.

Behold, He is coming with clouds, and every eye will see Him, even they who pierced Him. And all the tribes of the earth will mourn because of Him.[23]

The kingdoms of this world have become the kingdoms of our Lord and of His Christ, and He shall reign forever and ever![24]

And being found in appearance as a man, He humbled Himself and became obedient to the point of death, even the death of the cross. Therefore God also has highly exalted Him and given Him the name which is above every name, that at the name of Jesus every knee should bow, of those in heaven, and of those on earth, and of those under the earth, and that every tongue should confess that Jesus Christ is Lord, to the glory of God the Father.[25]

How can you not love a Lord like that? How can you not bow the knee to a God like that? How can you not allow this radiant Lord to capture your heart and ravish your soul? How can you not make Him your life's pursuit for the rest of your days on this earth?

And how can you preach and teach anything else?

Look again at the craftsman from Nazareth. Bow before Him, embrace Him, adore Him, and seek to know Him. He is available and closer to you than you can imagine. Jesus is your new tabernacle and temple. If you really want to see God present, dwelling among you, if you genuinely want to worship God in all of His glory, if you *truly* want to receive that gift of wonder and see glimpses of divine glory, then come to Him. Take your chances with the God of second chances. Jesus didn't die just to take you out of hell and into heaven. He died to take Himself out of heaven and deposit Himself into *you*.

STANDING ON A NEW FRONTIER

Today we stand on the edge of a new frontier—one of exploration, not fortification. One of discovery, not contentment. In this new frontier, we will navigate the unchartered waters of Jesus Christ, our all-sufficient Lord.[26] There is so much more of Christ to sail than we could ever imagine.

But if the truth be told, we have been handed a shrink-wrapped Jesus. Christ has become our once-a-week Mascot. We rally around Him on Sunday mornings, selfishly reaching for all we can get from Him—goodies and gifts, all for us. Then we push Him off to the sidelines the rest of the week.

But the game has never been about us; it's always been about Him.

The gospel that's so often preached today lacks a revelation of Jesus Christ. The contemporary gospel boils down to a fire-insurance policy, a Santa Claus God, or a performance-based religion. As long as we stay on that plane, we'll never see or comprehend the staggering enormity of our Lord.

Paul of Tarsus was a man who caught a glimpse of the excellencies of Jesus Christ. He preached such a high gospel that it turned illiterate, immoral pagans into full-pledged followers of Jesus who learned to live in authentic community—all in just a few months.[27]

What Paul did is something that our modern gospel could never pull off.

Only a recovery of the greatness, supremacy, sovereignty, brilliance, and "allness" of Christ will lead us to restoration and even revival. The wonder of Jesus as "all in all" is the only hope for igniting the flame of a new reformation and resuscitating a church that's presently on life support.

The body of Christ is in dire need of a reconversion to Jesus, not as Savior and Lord, but as the awe-inspiring, all-inclusive person He is. To say that He is our Savior and Lord is correct, of course, but it's inadequate. He is so much more. Christ is:

> your Shepherd, your Advocate, your Mediator, your Bridegroom, your Conqueror, your Lion, your Lamb, your sacrifice, your manna, your smitten Rock, your living water, your food, your drink, your good and abundant land, your dwelling place, your Sabbath, your new moon, your Jubilee, your new wine, your feast, your aroma, your anchor, your wisdom, your peace, your comfort, your Healer, your joy, your glory, your power, your strength, your wealth, your victory, your redemption, your Prophet, your Priest, your kinsman redeemer, your teacher, your guide, your liberator, your deliverer, your Prince, your Captain, your vision, your sight, your beloved, your way, your truth, your life, your author, your finisher, your beginning, your end, your age, your eternity—your all and all.

He is the same yesterday, today, and forever; yet He is new every morning. But beyond all of this, He is your King, your judge, and the True Witness.[28]

May God have a people on this earth who are of Christ, through Christ, and for Christ.

> O Christ, my life,
> possess me utterly.
> Take me and make a
> little Christ of me.
>
> —George McDonald,
> *Diary of an Old Soul* [29]

A people of the cross.

A people consumed with an unvarnished vision of God's eternal passion: to make Christ preeminent, supreme, and the head over all things visible and invisible.

A people who have discovered the touch of the Almighty in the face of His glorious Son, Jesus.

A people who wish to know only Christ and Him crucified, and to let everything else fall by the wayside.

A people who are searching His immeasurable depths, exploring His unfathomable heights, discovering His unsearchable riches, encountering His abundant life, receiving His infinite love, and making *Him* known to others.

In a world that sings, "Oh, who is this Jesus?" and a church that sings, "Oh, let's all be *like* Jesus," may we be a people who will sing with lungs of leather, "Oh, how we love Jesus!"

Though we have never discussed any of these issues, the two of us might disagree about many things—ecclesiology, eschatology, soteriology, economics, globalism, or politics. But in this book, we have sounded forth a united trumpet. We have sought to present the vision that has captured our hearts and that we wish to impart to the body of Christ—we have said in unison, "*One thing* [we] know . . ." [30] and that "one thing" is Jesus the Christ. He is the root and essence of Christianity. For that reason . . .

Christians don't follow Christianity;
they follow Christ.

Christians don't preach themselves;
they proclaim Christ.

Christians don't preach about Christ:
they simply preach Christ.

Christians don't shout from the rooftops, "Come to church";
they shout from the mountains, "Jesus Christ is born—come to
Christ!"

Christians don't point people to core values;
they point them to the incarnated, crucified, resurrected,
ascended, enthroned, exalted, triumphant, glorified,
reigning Lord—Jesus of Nazareth, the King, the
Messiah—the Christ beyond the tomb.

☩

It is with a burning heart for Jesus Christ and a guarded jealousy for His preeminence that we have written this book. We have written it for Him and to Him. We trust that it has been by Him and through Him.

We would give up everything we've ever written to have penned this one verse, a stanza that comes as close as is humanly possible to capturing the splendor of who Jesus is. It was written by Charles Wesley in 1739, with the music provided a century later by Felix Mendelssohn in a composition celebrating Johannes Gutenberg's gift of the printing press to planet Earth:

> *Hail the heaven-born Prince of Peace!*
> *Hail the Son of Righteousness!*
> *Light and life to all He brings,*
> *Risen with healing in His wings,*
> *Mild He lays His glory by,*
> *Born that man no more may die,*
> *Born to raise the sons of earth;*
> *Born to give them second birth.*
> *Hark! The herald angels sing,*
> *Glory to the newborn King!*[31]

This glorious One, Jesus the Christ, is our Pursuit, our Passion, and our Pleasure.[32] May He be so to you also.

AFTERWORD

A Personal Letter from Your Lord

Get alone in a quiet place, and read this letter with an open heart toward your Lord. May it mark a new day in your spiritual journey and draw you to love, adore, worship, and exalt the Lover of your soul, Christ Jesus.

Dear _____ [insert your name]

I am going to give you the complete knowledge of My Father's will, along with spiritual wisdom and understanding, so that the way you live will always honor and please Me, and your life will produce every kind of good fruit. All the while, you will grow as you learn to know Me better and better.

I will strengthen you with all My glorious power so you will have all the endurance and patience you need. And you will be filled with My joy, always thanking My Father.

My Father has enabled you to share in the inheritance that belongs to all of My people, those who live in the light, by rescuing you from the kingdom of darkness and transferring you into My Kingdom. I, dearly beloved of My Father, purchased your freedom and forgave you of all of your sins.

I am the visible image of the invisible God. I existed before anything was created, and I am supreme over all creation, for through Me, My Father created everything in the heavenly realms and on earth.

I made the things you can see and the things you cannot see—such as thrones, kingdoms, rulers, and authorities in the unseen world. Everything was created through Me and for Me.

I existed before anything else, and I hold all creation together.

I am the head of the church, which is My body.

I am the beginning, supreme over all who rise from the dead. So I am first in everything.

God in all His fullness was pleased to live in Me, and through Me God reconciled everything to Himself.

I made peace with everything in heaven and on earth by means of My blood on the cross.

This includes you who were once far away from God. You were His enemy, separated from Him by your evil thoughts and actions. Yet now My Father has reconciled you to Himself through My physical death. As a result, He has brought you into

His own presence, and you are holy and blameless as you stand before Him without a single fault.

Continue to believe this truth, and stand firmly in it. Don't drift away from the assurance you received when you heard the good news.

This message was kept secret for centuries and generations past, but now it has been revealed to you, for My Father wanted you to know that My riches and glory are for you. And this is the secret: *I live in you*. This gives you assurance of sharing My glory.

I am God's mysterious plan. In Me lie hidden all the treasures of wisdom and knowledge.

And now, just as you have accepted Me as your Lord, continue to follow Me. Let your roots grow down into Me, and let your life be built on Me. Then your faith will grow strong in the truth you were taught, and you will overflow with thankfulness.

Don't let anyone capture you with empty philosophies and high-sounding nonsense that come from human thinking and from the spiritual powers of this world, rather than from Me. In Me lives all the fullness of God in a human body, so you also are complete through your union with Me. I am the head over every ruler and authority.

You were once dead because of your sins, and your sinful nature was not yet cut away. Yet when you came to Me, you were "circumcised," but not by a physical procedure. I performed a spiritual circumcision on you—the cutting away of your sinful nature. You were buried with Me when you were baptized, and with Me you were raised to new life because you trusted the mighty power of God, who resurrected Me from the dead. My Father made you alive with Me, when He forgave all your sins. He canceled the record of the charges against you and took it away by nailing it to My cross. In this way, I disarmed the spiritual rulers and authorities. I shamed them publicly by My victory over them on the cross.

So don't let anyone condemn you for what you eat or drink, or for not celebrating certain holy days or new moon ceremonies or Sabbaths. These rules are only shadows of the reality which has come. And I am that reality. Don't let anyone condemn you by insisting on pious self-denial or the worship of angels, saying they have had visions about these things. Their sinful minds have made them proud, and they are not connected to Me, the head of the body. I hold the whole body together with its joints and ligaments, and it grows as My Father nourishes it.

You have died with me, and I have set you free from the spiritual powers of this world. "Don't handle! Don't taste! Don't touch!"? Such rules are mere human teachings about things that deteriorate as they are used. They may seem wise because they require strong devotion, pious self-denial, and severe bodily discipline. But they provide no help in conquering a person's evil desires.

Since you have been raised to new life with Me, set your sights on the realities of heaven, where I sit in the place of honor at My Father's right hand. Think about the things of heaven, not the things of earth, for you died to this life, and your real life is hidden with Me in God. And when I, your life, am revealed to the whole world, you will share in My glory.

Since My Father chose you to be a holy person He loves,

clothe yourself with tenderhearted mercy, kindness, humility, gentleness, and patience. Make allowance for other people's faults, and forgive anyone who offends you. Remember, I forgave you, so you, too, forgive others. Above all, clothe yourself with love, which binds you together with others in the church in perfect harmony. And let the peace that comes from Me rule in your heart, for as a member of My one body, you are called to live in peace. And always be thankful.

Let My message, in all its richness, fill your life. Teach and counsel others with all the wisdom I give. Sing psalms, hymns, and spiritual songs to My Father, with a thankful heart. And whatever you do or say, do it as My representative, giving thanks through Me to God the Father.

With unfailing and unconditional love,
Your Lord, Jesus the Christ

*Adapted from Colossians 1:9–3:16 NLT

NOTES

Introduction: "Who Do You Say That I Am?"

1. Hebrews 6:18–20 shows us that Jesus is the anchor of our souls. In Colossians 1:15–18, Paul wrote that all things hold together in Him.
2. Matt. 16:15, emphasis added.
3. John 12:32.
4. John 1:18; 1 John 4:9.
5. John 21:15–17.
6. See Exodus 20:7 and Deuteronomy 5:11.
7. Ludwig Wittgenstein, *Tractatus Logico-Philosophicus*, with an introduction by Bertrand Russell (New York: Routledge, 2002), 184 (German), 185 (English).
8. See Ludwig Wittgenstein, *Philosophical Investigations*, a German text, with English translation by G. E. M. Anscombe, P. M. S. Hacker, and Joachim Schulte, rev. 4th ed. (West Sussex, UK / Malden, MA: Wiley-Blackwell, 2009), part II, xi (204c).
9. Ludwig Wittgenstein, *Last Writings on Philosophy and Psychology: Preliminary Studies* (Oxford: Basil Blackwell, 1982), 1: 61–65, 68–69, 90, 97.
10. As recorded by the editor in the epilogue to Karl Barth, *Fragments Grave and Gay*, ed. Martin Rumscheidt (London: Collins, 1971), 124.

11. "Jesus Loves Me" was written by Anna B. Warner in 1860. See also the words of two other nineteenth-century hymns: "There is a Name I love to hear / I love to sing its worth / It sounds like music in my ear / The sweetest name on earth / O, how I love Jesus . . . because he first loved me!" from Frederick Whitfield, "O How I Love Jesus," written in 1855; and "My Jesus, I love thee / I know thou art mine; . . . / If ever I loved thee, my Jesus, 'tis now," written by William R. Featherstone in 1864.

12. Paraphrased.

13. 1 John 4:17.

14. John 3:16.

15. See 1 John 4:9.

16. See 2 Corinthians 3:3 and Matthew 5:13–16.

17. Or, in English, *Summary of Theology*, or *Highest Theology*. Following a supernatural encounter, Aquinas said, "I can write no more; compared with what I have seen, all I have written seems to me as straw." (Peter, Kreeft, ed., *A Shorter Summa: The Essential Philosophical Passages of St. Thomas Aquinas' Summa Theologica* [San Francisco: Ignatius Press, 1993], 37).

18. 1 Tim. 6:15; Rev. 19:16.

Chapter 1: The Occupation of All Things

1. This biblical text inspired what we consider to be one of the greatest hymns ever written, Charles Wesley's 1734 "Hark! The Herald Angels Sing." The third verse begins, "Hail the heaven-born Prince of Peace! Hail the Sun of Righteousness! Light and life to all he brings, risen with healing in his wings."

2. Dietrich Bonhoeffer, *Christ the Center: A New Translation*, trans. Edwin H. Robertson (San Francisco: HarperSanFrancisco, 1978), 60–65.

3. An oft-quoted saying attributed to H. G. Wells, possibly from late in his life.

4. See Revelation 22:16.

5. Phil. 3:10; John 14:9; Heb. 8:11; 1 John 2:20, 27.

6. 1 Cor. 1:9. Our faith is what the ancients called *pistis christou*, "faith in Christ," or alternatively translated "the faithfulness of Christ."

7. The first line of John Henry Newman's familiar hymn; the original poem was titled "The Pillar of the Cloud." See his *Selected Sermons, Prayers, and Devotions*, eds. John F. Thornton and Susan B. Varenne (New York: Vintage, 1999), 347.

8. Matt. 3:17.

9. Matt. 17:5. See also 1 John 5:9.

10. Matt. 12:34.

11. Matt. 4:4.

12. John 1:1, 14; 1 John 1:1–4, 14. See also John 17:5, 24 and Philippians 2:6.

13. John 1:18 NLT. See also Hebrews 1:1–2.

14. In the New Testament, we sometimes see the Spirit revealing a person's calling or some future event. But both of these reveal Christ. Jesus Christ is the Omega; He is the future. And revealing one's calling is simply revealing what spiritual part that individual will play in Christ's body, to express Christ Himself.

15. John 15:26.

16. John 16:13–15.

17. See John 16:8–11.

18. Also, the "spirit of prophecy," which many take as a reference to the Holy Spirit, testifies of Jesus (Rev. 19:10).

19. Col. 2:9.

20. Col. 1:19.

21. See also Luke 2:12–14; 4:10; Mark 1:13; John 1:51; 1 Peter 3:22; 2 Thess. 1:7.

22. Col. 1:16–17; See also John 1:3; 1 Corinthians 8:6; Romans 11:36.

23. Eph. 1:10.

24. John 8:12.

25. John 4:10; 7:38.

26. Death means separation. Gen. 1:9–13; 1 Cor. 15:4.

27. John 15:1; 6:57.

28. John 12:24; 6:35.

29. Mal. 4:2.

30. Col. 2:16–17.

31. 2 Peter 1:19; Rev. 22:16.

32. John 1:29. See also Revelation 5.

33. Rom. 5:14; 1 Cor. 15:47.

34. Col. 2:16–17.

35. Rom. 8:19–23; Eph. 4:10.

36. From *Divine Hymns, or Spiritual Songs*, a collection by Joshua Smith and others, 8th ed., 1797, hymn II, reprinted in N. H. Allen, "Old Time Music and Musicians," *Connecticut Quarterly* 3 (1897): 68.

37. John 5:39 NLT.

38. Luke 24:27, 31 NIV.

39. Luke 24:44–45 NIV.

40. Matt. 2:15. See Hosea 11:1.

41. Gal. 3:16. See also Isaiah 49.

42. See Deuteronomy 8:3; 6:13, 16.

43. For details, see Frank Viola, *From Eternity to Here: Rediscovering the Ageless Purpose of God* (Colorado Springs: David C. Cook, 2009), 23–222 (parts 1 and 2).

44. Rom. 5:14.

45. 1 Cor. 15:45, 47.

46. Eph. 5:31–32.

47. Emphasis added. See also Hebrews 8:4; 1 Peter 1:10–11.

48. For a scholarly treatment of every New Testament text that quotes or alludes to the Old Testament, see G. K. Beale and D. A. Carson's 1,239-page *Commentary on the New Testament Use of the Old Testament* (Grand Rapids: Baker Academic, 2007).

49. For details, see Frank Viola, "Beyond Bible Study: Finding Jesus Christ in Scripture," www.ptmin.org/beyond.pdf.

50. John Calvin, *Commentary on the Gospel According to John* (Grand Rapids: Eerdmans, 1956), 1:218.

51. Charles H. Spurgeon, "Christ Precious to Believers," sermon 23, in *Sermons Preached and Revised by Rev. C. H. Spurgeon*, 6th series (New York: Sheldon, 1860), 357.

52. Acts 3:20.

53. Acts 8:5.

54. Acts 9:20. See also Acts 17:3.

55. 1 John 1:1–3.

56. Acts 5:42 KJV.

57. Sören Kierkegaard, *Philosophical Fragments*, chapter 4, available online at Religion Online, "Philosophical Fragments of Sören Kierkegaard," http://www.religion-online.org/showbook.asp?title=2512. We thank our friend Alan Hirsch for pointing us to this quote.

58. One of us also obsessively looks at the indexes of books not permeated with references to Jesus, to see if Jesus is even referenced at all or deemed worthy of indexing.

59. Matt. 12:34. See also Luke 6:45.

60. Eph. 3:8.

61. Col. 1:28 NASB.

62. Gal. 1:16.

63. 2 Cor. 4:5.

64. Samuel J. Stone (1838–1900), "The Church's One Foundation," verse 1.

65. Matt. 16:15–17. See also Luke 10:22.

66. Gal. 1:15–16. See also verse 12.

67. Rom. 16:25.

68. Eph. 1:16–17 NIV.

69. See Luke 24:32.

70. 2 Cor. 4:6.

71. Jesus said, "Out of the abundance of the heart his mouth speaks" (Luke 6:45). Obviously, the consistent fruit of a person's life is also an indicator of what he or she is occupied with.

72. Watchman Nee, *Christ the Sum of All Spiritual Things* (New York: Christian Fellowship Publishers, 1973), 8.

73. T. Austin-Sparks, "Our Ministry," July 1942, Lighthouse Library, http://www.lighthouselibrary.com/read.php?sel=4008&searchfor=%7C%7C&type=&what=title.

74. From Helen H. Lemmel's "Turn Your Eyes Upon Jesus" (refrain), available at http://my.homewithgod.com/heavenlymidis2/turneyes.html.

75. Phil. 3:12 KJV.

76. Kreeft, *A Shorter Summa*, 37.

77. George Morris, *The Mystery and Meaning of Christian Conversion* (Nashville: Discipleship Resources, 1981), 170.

78. J. C. Ryle, *Holiness* (Lafayette, IN: Sovereign Grace, 2001), 196. Ryle was appointed in 1880 as the first bishop of Liverpool by Prime Minister Benjamin Disraeli. A hundred years later, Jane Kenyon wrote similar thoughts in her poem "Looking at Stars," which appeared in her third volume of poetry, *Let Evening Come* (Saint Paul: Graywolf Press, 1990, p. 67): "The God of curved space, the dry. God is not going to help us, but the son whose blood spattered the hem of his mother's robe."

Chapter 2: A Bottle in the Ocean

1. Phil. 3:7–8 NIV.

2. We are aware that some scholars contest Pauline authorship of Colossians. However, we agree with those scholars who support Pauline authorship, which was never debated until the nineteenth century. For details on this discussion, see Donald Guthrie, *New Testament Introduction* (Downers Grove, IL: InterVarsity Press, 1990), 572–77.

3. This book was conceived in the midst of a conversation about our mutual love for Colossians and how its incredible presentation of Christ has been lost today.

4. Col. 2:8–23.

5. Col. 2:19.

6. Col. 2:8.

7. See Colossians 1:13–14.

8. Col. 2:9.

9. Col. 1:14–18.

10. We love the language of "carpenter" for Jesus. It summons up a bouquet of fragrant songs, paintings, and stories. But the actual Greek word is *tekton*, which really means "craftsman," "artisan," or "builder." In Jesus' day, this would make Him more a mason than anything. There was not much wood in His region to work with, even then. The house Jesus lived in at Nazareth was stone and mud, for example, not wood. Most likely, as a *tekton*, Jesus spent no more than 10–20 percent of His time working with wood; the rest, with stone and rocks. Hence the power of His stone metaphors. From now on we shall use the word "craftsman" instead of "carpenter," hoping that you will not lose the bouquet.

11. Col. 1:27. See also John 1:16.

12. Col. 3:4, emphasis added.

13. Col. 2:10.
14. Col. 2:1–5.
15. Col. 2:6–7 NASB.
16. 1 Cor. 3:16; Eph. 2:21–22; 1 Peter 2:5.
17. See Matthew 3:17; 12:18; 17:5; Mark 1:11; and Luke 3:22.
18. Col. 2:16.
19. Col. 2:15.
20. Col. 3:15.
21. Col. 3:16.
22. The Greek word for "dwell" (*enoikeo*) means to "live in."
23. Col. 3:17.
24. Col. 2:14. See also Romans 7; 10:4; Ephesians 2:15; Galatians 4:1–7;
    Hebrews 8–10.
25. Col. 3:16–17.
26. Col. 3:18.
27. Col. 4:1.
28. Col. 4:7.
29. Col. 4:17.
30. 1 Tim. 1:3.
31. Luke 24:31.
32. Eph. 3:8.
33. Ora Rowan (1834–1879), "Hast Thou Heard Him, Seen Him, Known
    Him?" *Christian Worship* (Exeter, Eng.: Paternoster Press, 1976), 689.

Chapter 3: If God Wrote Your Biography

1. One of the implications of this is that you cannot have a spiritual experience
   that Jesus Christ has not already had Himself. You are "in Christ," which
   means His history is your history, and His destiny is your destiny.
2. 2 Cor. 3:3.
3. Eph. 1:4.
4. In Ephesians 1:5, the word "predestined" (*proorizo*) literally means
   "marked out beforehand."
5. Col. 1:17.
6. The words "born again" in John 3:7 literally mean "born again," or "born
   anew," but the "more relevant meaning" of the Greek ανωθεν (*anōthen*) as
   used here is "from above." (D. Moody Smith, *John: Abingdon New
   Testament Commentaries* [Nashville: Abingdon Press, 1999], 95.)
7. John 3:7 CEV.
8. 1 Peter 1:23; some versions do use "born anew" here.
9. 1 John 5:1 NRSV.
10. John 11:25.
11. 1 John 5:20. See also verses 11–12.

12. 2 Peter 1:3–4.

13. 2 Cor. 4:18.

14. Heb. 2:9. See also 2 Corinthians 3:18.

15. Rev. 3:20.

16. Rev. 3:22.

17. Heb. 6:4.

18. 1 Peter 2:3. See also Hebrews 6:5.

19. Col. 2:19.

20. 2 Cor. 2:14.

21. Col. 2:13; Eph. 2:5.

22. 2 Cor. 5:17.

23. Gal. 4:19.

24. Eph. 4:20.

25. Eph. 4:15.

26. 1 Cor. 3:1; 1 Peter 2:2.

27. 1 Cor. 13:11.

28. Rom. 8:19, 23; Eph. 1:5; Gal. 4:5; Heb. 2:10.

29. See Hebrews 5:12–14.

30. 1 Cor. 1:30.

31. 2 Peter 1:4.

32. 1 Cor. 2:16.

33. Gal. 2:20.

34. Rom. 6:6 NASB.

35. Col. 2:20.

36. Phil. 3:10.

37. 2 Cor. 4:10–12; Luke 9:23–24; Col. 3:5–8; Rom. 8:13.

38. Rom. 6:4.

39. Col. 2:12.

40. The following texts speak about the world system: John 17:16; 1 Cor. 2:12; Gal. 1:4; 6:14; Eph. 2:2; Titus 2:12; James 1:27; 4:4; 2 Peter 1:4; 2:20; 1 John 2:15–17; 5:4–5.

41. Col. 2:12.

42. Col. 3:1.

43. Eph. 2:6.

44. Mark 16:17–18; Luke 9:1; 10:19; 2 Cor. 10:3–5; Eph. 1:20–21; 6:11–18.

45. Paul used the phrase "in Christ" more than two hundred times in his letters. Vital union with Jesus Christ is a dominant theme in the apostle's writings.

46. Rom. 8:30.

47. Hebrews 4:4 NIV.

48. Gen. 2:1; John 5:36; 17:4; 19:30; Rom. 9:28; Heb. 12:2.

49. Eph. 4:11–16.

50. Tod Bolsinger gets credit for this phrase. See his *It Takes a Church to*

Raise a Christian: How the Community of God Transforms Lives (Grand Rapids: Braznos Press, 2004).

51. Eph. 4:10.
52. Eph. 1:10.
53. Rom. 8:29.
54. Heb. 2:10.
55. Col. 3:4. See also 1 John 3:2 and 2 Thessalonians 1:10.
56. James 1:18.
57. Rom. 8:19.
58. Luke 2:52.
59. Eph. 4:13.
60. Eph. 1:22–23.
61. Heb. 12:2, emphasis added.
62. Heb. 6:20.
63. Eph. 3:11.
64. Quoted in "Ephrem the Syrian," http://thebyzantineanglocatholic. blogspot.com/2008/06/ephrem-syrian.html. See also Saint Ephrem, *Harp of the Spirit: Eighteen Poems of Saint Ephrem* (London: Fellowship of St. Alban and St. Sergius, 1983), 35.
65. For a detailed unfolding of God's eternal purpose, see Frank Viola, *From Eternity to Here* (Colorado Springs: David C. Cook, 2009).
66. Phil. 1:21.
67. 1 John 4:17.
68. Eph. 5:8.
69. As quoted by Ronald Blythe, *The Bookman's Tale* (London: Canterbury Press, 2009), 96–97. See the full prayer on UK's St. Edmundsburg Cathedral's Web page, http://www.stedscathedral.co.uk/.
70. 1 John 4:19.
71. Phil. 1:6.
72. Timothy Radcliffe, *Why Go to Church: The Drama of the Eucharist* (New York: Continuum, 2008), 157. See also Janet Martin Soskice, *The Kindness of God: Metapor, Gender, and Religious Language* (New York: Oxford University Press, 2007), 5.
73. 2 Cor. 3:3.

Chapter 4: A Violin Called Messiah

1. 2 Chron. 15:2.
2. Rev. 3:20.
3. Meister Eckhart, "The Kingdom of God Is at Hand" (sermon 69) in *The Works of Meister Eckhart, Doctor Ecstaticus*, ed. Franz Pfeifer (Kila, MT: Kessinger Publishing, n.d.), 171.
4. Gal. 4:19.

5. "Antonio Stradivari: Lord of the Strings," *Economist*, September 2, 2004, http://www.economist.com/printedition/displayStory.cfm?Story_ ID=3150810 (subscribers only). For more on Stradivari and the Messiah, see Toby Faber, *Stradivari's Genius: Five Violins, One Cello and Three Centuries of Enduring Perfection* (New York: Random House, 2004).

6. George Eliot, "Stradivarius," in her *Poems* (Boston: Estes and Lauriat, 1895), 2:175.

7. "Antonio Stradivari: Lord of the Strings."

8. Ibid.

9. 1 Cor. 11:1.

10. See Philippians 3:17: "Be ye imitators together of me" (ASV); "Join in imitating me" (RSV). "Join with others in following my example" (NIV), and "Join in following my example," (NKJV) don't cut it either.

11. Phil. 2:6–11.

12. Augustine, Sermon 27, in his *Sermons 20–50*, trans. Edmund Hill, *The Works of Saint Augustine: A Translation for the 21st Century* (Hyde Park, NY: New City Press, 2009), 107.

13. For another way of putting it, "The beating heart of the universe now beneath a human heart," see English literary critic Muriel C. Bradbrook (1909–1993), as quoted in Michael Mayne, *The Enduring Melody* (London: Darton, Longman & Todd, 2006), 179.

14. Col. 1:27.

15. Maria McKee on Nightmusic, "Breathe," *http://www.youtube.com/ watch?v=RvRxYty2ie0*.

16. Symeon the New Theologian, "We Awaken in Christ's Body," in *The Enlightened Heart: An Anthology of Sacred Poetry*, ed. Stephen Mitchell (New York: Harper and Row, 1989), 38–39.

17. 2 Cor. 5:14. In the NIV it also "compels us" but in the RSV it "controls us," and in the NRSV it merely "urges us on."

18. 1 Cor. 6:15–17.

19. Augustine, *Commentary on First John bk. 10, chap. 8*.

20. John 13:34 NIV.

21. John 15:13 NIV.

22. Meister Eckhart, *Treatises and Sermons*, trans. John Voss Skinner (New York: Harper, 1958), 157: "How should man know that he knows God, if he does not know himself."

23. 1 John 3:2.

24. Heb. 1:3 NIV.

25. Thx! to Kelly Ballard for getting us to think along these lines.

26. 2 Peter 1:4 NIV.

27. This quote is as Leonard remembers seeing it when he was teaching a course at Keble College.

28. Gal. 2:20.

29. 1 Cor. 2:16.

30. See Acts 17:28.

31. For more on Cupitt's refusing to see how a non-rational approach to God can be anything but irrational, see his *Above Us Only Sky: The Religion of Ordinary Life* (Santa Rosa, CA: Polebridge Press, 2008).

32. This translation of Colossians 3:5 comes from Robert Mulholland, *The Deeper Journey: The Spirituality of Discovering Your True Self* (Downers Grove, IL: InterVarsity, 2006), 63.

33. 2 Cor. 9:15.

34. The second stanza of James G. Small, "I've Found a Friend," written in the 1860s. See *Devotional Hymns: A Collection of Hymns and Songs for Use in All Services of the Church . . .* (Chicago: Hope Publishing Co., 1935), 200.

35. A friend of mine (Leonard) is a master woodworker. He is an Episcopal rector named Michael Blewett, and because of his love for his craft, he enjoys the metaphor of Jesus as our Story Stick.

    A story stick is a tool as old as woodworking. It is more reliable than a tape measure. It is made from a single strip of wood, and you can take it wherever. This one "story stick" contains all of the wood-carver's projects, with his critical measurements marked in full-scale proportion. In Michael's words, "Taken together, these marks present a precise visual representation, or story, of a project." One small stick can replicate a masterpiece. We are Christ's story stick. This is my story, and I'm sticking to it! For another account from Michael Blewett, see "The Window," April 2009, http://www.cecbg.com/news/April-2009.pdf.

36. Gal. 2:20 NIV.

37. For an incredible image of what it might be like for your life and mine when we manifest, not just mediate, Christ's presence, check out the YouTube video at http://www.youtube.com/watch?v=CcsSPzr7ays.

38. The concluding lines of Archibald MacLeish, "Ars Poetica," in his *Poems, 1924–1933* (Boston: Houghton Mifflin, 1933), 123.

39. Slavoj Žižek, *Violence: Six Sideways Reflections* (New York: Picador, 2008), 56.

40. John 1:14.

41. Col. 1:15.

42. Luke 1:46–55.

43. Heb. 12:2.

44. Paul used the words *Spirit of God* and *Spirit of Christ* without distinction and synonymously (Rom. 8:9).

45. Heb. 1:3.

46. Rev. 22:16.

47. See Colossians 1:2.

48. See Galatians 6:14 in the KJV or ASV.

Chapter 5: A Ditch on Either Side

1. Barth often wrote about the "razor edge" in his various writings.
2. Deut. 5:32.
3. John 14:6.
4. George MacDonald, "The Consuming Fire," in *Επεα [Epea] Aptera: Unspoken Sermons*, by George MacDonald and Robert Browning (London: A. Strahan, 1867; repr. Whitethorn, CA: Johannesen, 1997), 1:28.
5. See for example, John Rawls, *A Theory of Justice*, rev. ed. (Cambridge, MA: Belknap Press of Harvard University Press, 2000.) The grandson of social gospel theologian Walter Rauschenbush, Princeton professor Richard Rorty critiques Rawls's position in "Justice as a Larger Loyalty," *Cosmopolitics: Thinking and Feeling Beyond the Nation*, ed. Pheng Cheah (Minneapolis: University of Minnesota Press, 1998), 45–58.
6. Phil. 2:5.
7. In the words of the "the greatest British Jew of all time," a distinction bestowed on Rabbi Louis Jacobs just before his death in 2006, "There are many great figures in Judaism's long history, from Abraham, Moses, Isaiah, Rabbi Akiba, Maimonides, the Baal Shem Toy, the Vilna Gaon—the list is endless, but each of these is only a link in the chain—a very strong link, but a link nonetheless—and we too are links in the same golden chain." (Louis Jacobs, "Veyakhel," in his *Jewish Preaching: Homilies and Sermons* [Portland, OR: Vallentine Mitchell, 2004], 100.)
8. Jacob Neusner, *A Rabbi Talks with Jesus: An Intermillennial Interfaith Exchange* (New York: Doubleday, 1993), 152.
9. David Klinghoffer, *Why the Jews Rejected Jesus: The Turning Point in Western History* (New York: Doubleday, 2005), 47. For a similar verdict— "Our conclusion is therefore that the preaching of values and concrete norms in the New Testament is mostly not a new teaching but has rather a paranetic and maieutic task"—see Josef Fuchs, *Christian Ethics in a Secular Arena* (Washington, D.C.: Georgetown University Press, 1984), 22.
10. See especially Ezekiel 37.
11. If "person" were rightly understood, we wouldn't need to specify people. The symbol for the whole, integrated personality is "gathered together." The whole person is "gathered together," which means a gathering of what is outside and inside, a coming into one of relationships and attributes. But in a culture that worships "the self," we must name both person and people.
12. This oft-quoted saying of G. K. Chesterton may well come from his 1920s biography, *St. Francis of Assisi* (New York: Random House, 1990), 16, where he states that St. Francis's "religion was not a thing like a theory but a thing like a love-affair."

13. Shakespeare, *King Lear* (act 5, scene 3), in *The Complete Dramatic and Poetic Works of William Shakespeare*, ed. William Allan Neilson (Boston: Houghton, Mifflin, 1906), 1002.

14. Eph. 5:32 NRSV.

15. Col. 1:26–27; 2:2; Eph. 3:4–6; 5:32.

16. Rom. 16:25; 1 Cor. 2:7; Eph. 3:4, 10; Col. 1:26–7; 2:2–3; 4:3.

17. Col. 2:2 NRSV.

18. The Greek word is *anakephalaiosis*, signifying not just "recapitulation" but also the "work of Christ in becoming the head of a new humanity." See Justo L. González, *Essential Theological Terms* (Louisville: Westminster John Knox Press, 2005), 148.

19. Col. 1:20.

20. Richard Cross, *Duns Scotus on God* (Aldershot, UK: Ashgate, 2005), 8. For the origin of "dunce," check an unabridged dictionary.

21. For the "disenchantment of the world" that Max Weber saw accompanying the rise of science, see the various references in Sam Whimster, ed., *The Essential Weber: A Reader* (New York: Routledge, 2004).

22. 2 Cor. 5:7.

23. From *Introduction to the Book of Job* (1907), as quoted on the American Chester Society Web site, "Quotations of G.K. Chesterton," http:// chesterton.org/discover/quotations.html.

24. G. B. Caird, *Paul's Letters from Prison: Ephesians, Philippians, Colossians, Philemon, in the Revised Standard Version: The New Clarendon Bible* (New York: Oxford University Press, 1976), 70.

25. First presented at a meeting of the Los Angeles Psychoanalytic Society and Institute, 12 October 1985, this excerpt, by the late Clifford Scott, is as quoted in Manfred F. R. Kets de Vries, *Leaders, Fools, and Imposters: Essays on the Psychology of Leadership*, rev. ed. (New York: iUniverse, 2003), 27.

26. Ex. 33:21–33.

27. Luke 8:43–44.

28. 1 Cor. 13:12.

29. Col. 2:9.

30. Rom. 11:33.

31. Thomas à Kempis, *The Imitation of Christ in Four Books* (book 3, ch. 56), trans. Richard Challoner (Dublin: James Duffy, 1842), 364.

32. See "Threshold Five: Entering the Kingdom," in Don Everts and Doug Schaupp, *I Once Was Lost: What Postmodern Skeptics Taught Us about Their Path to Jesus* (Downers Grove, IL: IVP Books, 2008), 103–18; see also Leonard Sweet, *Out of the Question, Into the Mystery: The Godlife Relationship* (Colorado Springs: Waterbrook Press, 2004).

33. Tryon Edwards, *A Dictionary of Thoughts: Being a Cyclopedia of Laconic Quotations from the Best Authors of the World, Both Ancient and Modern* (Detroit: F. B. Dickerson, 1908), 369.

34. Col. 3:11.
35. 1 Cor. 2:2.
36. 1 Cor. 1:30.
37. 1 Cor. 1:24, 30.
38. Eph. 2:14.
39. John 14:6.
40. 1 Cor. 1:24.

Chapter 6: His Face or Your Face?

1. Charles Arnold-Baker's definition of "political correctness" is our favorite: "the insistence upon something which is not correct except, depending on the point of view, in a political sense." (Charles Arnold-Baker, *The Companion to British History*, 3rd ed. [Battle, Eng.: Loncross Denholm Press, 2009]. Quoted in Alex Burghart, "A Rare Friend," *TLS: Times Literary Supplement*, 27 March 2009, 24.)
2. Brother François of Taizé, "Why Brother Roger Died," Taizé Community, http://www.taize.fr/en_article3790.html.
3. Rev. 2:4.
4. 1 John 4:17.
5. See its classic formulation in the social gospel drawn from Sunday sermons preached by Charles M. Sheldon and fictionalized in his *In His Steps* (Nashville: Broadman Press, 1896), with the latest edition being an e-book published in 2009 (Escondido, CA: Christian Audio, 2009).
6. See Matthew 5:17, where Jesus was in essence saying, "Don't misunderstand why I have come. I did not come to abolish the law of Moses or the writings of the prophets. No, I came to fulfill them." Likewise, He did not come to abolish you but to fulfill you.
7. Rom. 6:6–14; Col. 3:5–17.
8. Jean Danielou, "Le Symbolisme des Rites Baptismaux," *Dieu Vivant* 1 (1945): 17, as translated by Robert Taft and quoted in his *The Liturgy of the Hours in East and West: The Origins of the Divine Office and Its Meaning for Today* (Collegeville, MN: Liturgical Press, 1985), 371.
9. John 10:30.
10. John 20:21.
11. John 15:9.
12. John 5:19 NLT.
13. John 20:17 NRSV.
14. The Greek is "*ekstasis*," meaning one steps out of himself. Hence the real meaning of "ecstasy" or "ecstatic."
15. Gal. 2:20 NRSV.
16. John Milton, *Paradise Lost* (New York: Penguin Putnam, 2003), 123 (book 5, line 869).

17. Quoted in Matthew Woodley, *Holy Fools: Following Jesus with Reckless Abandon* (Carol Stream, IL: Tyndale, 2008), 148.

18. CBA (Christian Booksellers Association) is the trade association for the Christian Retail Channel (http://www.cbaonline.org/).

19. Gene Edward Veith, "You Are What You Read," *World Magazine*, 7 July 2002, 26–34, http://www.worldmag.com/articles/19.

20. Philippians 3:12: "Not that I have already attained, or am already perfected; but I press on, that I may lay hold of that for which Christ Jesus has also laid hold of me."

21. Robert F. Taft, *Through Their Own Eyes: Liturgy as the Byzantines Saw It* (Berkeley, CA: InterOrthodox Press, 2007), 136.

22. But it's not the same secret that author Rhonda Byrne shared with the world in her self-help film and subsequent book, both titled *The Secret*.

23. Col. 1:27.

24. "Apostolic Letter Novo Millennio Ineunte of His Holiness Pope John Paul II to the Bishops, Clergy and the Lay Faithful at the Close of the Great Jubilee of the Year 2000," section 2:16–28, http://www.vatican.va/holy_father/john_paul_ii/apost_letters/documents/hf_jp-ii_apl_20010106_novo-millennio-ineunte_en.html. Quoted in Benedict XVI, *The Apostles* (Huntington, IN: Our Sunday Visitor, 2007), 9.

25. 1 Peter 1:8.

26. 2 Cor. 3:18.

27. Gerard Manly Hopkins, "Christ Our Hero," in his *Sermons and Devotional Writings* (New York: Oxford University Press, 1959), 35.

28. Col. 2:9.

29. 2 Cor. 5:16–17.

30. Our thanks to Vange Thiessen for this story (26 October 2004).

Chapter 7: A Collision of Two Empires

1. Ravi Zacharias, www.rzim.org.

2. Eph. 1:22. See also Ephesians 4:15; 5:23; Colossians 1:18.

3. Frederick William Faber's hymn "There's a Wideness in God's Mercy," written in 1854.

4. See Note 6 of chapter 9.

5. Heb. 1:2.

6. "Apostolic Journey of His Holiness Benedict XVI to Brazil on the Occasion of the Fifth General Conference of the Bishops of Latin America and the Caribbean, Inaugural Session of the Fifth General Conference of the Bishops of Latin America and the Caribbean," http://www.vatican.va/holy_father/benedict_xvi/speeches/2007/may/documents/hf_ben-xvi_spe_20070513_conference-aparecida_en.html. This was the opening speech at Latin American bishops' general conference in Aparecida, Brazil, May 2007.

7. John 8:12.

8. Richard Finn, *Almsgiving in the Later Roman Empire* (New York: Oxford University Press, 2006), 182, 264.

9. Eamon Duffy, *Walking to Emmaus* (New York: Burns & Oates, 2006), 56.

10. Matt. 6:33.

11. It seems strange to us that those most into "social justice" are those least into justice theories of the atonement, where God's justice demanded a sacrifice.

12. Rob Miller ("Roblimo"), "Wikipedia Founder Jimmy Wales Responds," *Slashdot*, 28 July 2004, http://interviews.slashdot.org/article. pl?sid=04/07/28/1351230. Reprinted in Brian T. Chatfield, *The Complete Guide to Wikis: How to Set Up, Use, and Benefit from Wikis for Teachers, Business Professionals, Families, and Friends* (Ocala, FL: Atlantic Publishing, 2009), 17. See also Andrew Lih, *The Wikipedia Revolution: How a Bunch of Nobodies Created the World's Greatest Encyclopedia* (London: Aurum Press, 2009).

13. The third and fourth phrases of the first stanza of Charles Wesley, "Hark! The Herald Angels Sing," written in 1734.

14. Reinhold Niebuhr, *The Irony of American History* (New York: Charles Scribner & Sons, 1952; repr., University of Chicago Press, 2008), 160.

15. His name is synonymous with the best in Greek study Bibles.

16. Luke 1:46–55.

17. Matt. 5:7.

18. Luke 6:36.

19. Matt. 18:22–35.

20. However, he added that there was just something about music. Perhaps, he mused, music had something to do with the second good idea coming into the world. (Kurt Vonnegut, *Palm Sunday: An Autobiographical Collage* [New York: Delacorte, 1981], 325.)

21. Strategist Faris Yakob calls it this. For more see http://farisyakob.typepad. com/blog/2008/11/interesting-a-history-of-recombinant-culture.html.

22. This was an Apple advertising slogan.

23. St. Peter Chrysologus, as quoted in Thomas J. Norris, *The Trinity: Life of God, Hope for Humanity: Towards a Theology of Communion* (Hyde Park, NY: New City Press, 2009), 105. Or in another translation: "Therefore, come, return and at least thus have experience of Me as a Father whom you see returning good things for evils, love for injuries, such great charities for such great wounds," Sermon 108: "Man as Both a Priest and a Sacrifice to God," in Ludwig Schopp, ed., *Saint Peter Chrysologus Saint Valerian: Selected Sermons; Homilies: The Fathers of the Church: A New Translation*, vol. 17 (New York: Fathers of the Church, 1953).

24. We are aware that some people called Jesus demon-possessed, even the "chief of Beelzebub." But we forget that His disciples wondered about this at times as well. In Mark 8:32, Peter "began to rebuke" Jesus for His crazy talk about a becoming a "suffering messiah," which was an oxymoron for good Jews like Peter. The Greek for "rebuke" here connotes exorcising a

demon, so it's as if Peter was trying to "rebuke" or cast out Jesus' "misunderstanding" of the Messiah's mission. Jesus turned the tables on Peter and "rebuked" (same word) him for being demon-possessed: "Get behind Me, Satan!" He said. (The tempter did not just appear to Jesus once in His mission. He came even through Jesus' own friends. And like Jesus, we, too, live with the tempter all the time. But satan ought not to be in our line of vision, just in our shadow. Let's get him behind us!)

25. John MacMurray, *Persons in Relation* (New York: Harper, 1961), 171.

26. Rev. 5:5; 22:16.

27. Eph. 1:23.

28. Acts 7:52.

29. Acts 2:27.

30. John 18:36.

31. Isa. 49:2.

32. Ps. 84:9.

33. See David Klinghoffer, *Why the Jews Rejected Jesus: The Turning Point in Western History* (New York: Doubleday, 2005), 102.

34. Here are a few representative titles from their massive lists of publications: John Howard Yoder: *The Politics of Jesus: Vicit Agnus Noster*, 2nd ed. (Grand Rapids: Eerdmans, 1994); *Body Politics: Five Practices of the Christian Community Before the Watching World* (Scottdale, PA: Herald Press, 2001); *Discipleship as Political Responsibility* (Scottdale, PA: Herald Press, 2003). Stanley Hauerwas: *After Christendom? How the Church Is to Behave If Freedom, Justice, and a Christian Nation Are Bad Ideas* (Nashville: Abingdon, 1999); *A Better Hope: Resources for a Church Confronting Capitalism, Democracy and Postmodernity* (Grand Rapids: Brazos Press, 2000); *Living Gently in a Violent World: The Prophetic Witness of Weakness* (Downers Grove, IL: IVP Press, 2008).

35. Benedict XVI, *John Paul II: My Beloved Predecessor* (Boston: Pauline Books & Media, 2007), 20.

36. George Weigel, *Witness of Hope: The Biography of Pope John Paul II* (New York: HarperCollins, 1999).

Chapter 8: The Forgotten Tree

1. C. S. Lewis, *Mere Christianity: A Revised and Amplified Edition, with a New Introduction, of the Three Books, Broadcast Talks, Christian Behaviour, and Beyond Personality* [bk. 3, chap. 11] (San Francisco: HarperSanFrancisco, 2001), 142.

2. John 5:19.

3. John 5:30.

4. Matt. 19:16–17.

5. John 5:19 NIV.

6. John 5:30 NIV.

7. John 8:28 NIV.

8. John 12:49 NIV.

9. John 14:10 NIV.

10. John 15:5, emphasis added.

11. John 20:17.

12. Matt. 27:50–51.

13. Heb. 10:19–20.

14. Heb. 4:10.

15. 1 Thess. 5:24.

16. Phil. 2:13.

17. John 15:1; 6:57 KJV.

18. We are not defining "religion" the way the apostle James did in James 1. There the word *religion* means "worship." We are instead using the word to mean a system of human thought, belief, and practice that typically involves a higher power.

19. The sixth verse of Henry Baker's nineteenth-century hymn "Lord, Thy Word Abideth," *Christian Worship* (Exeter, UK: Paternoster Press, 1976), 289.

20. Matt. 11:19; Luke 7:34.

21. Interestingly, Jesus grew up in a poor family in rural Galilee. And He was no doubt Himself ostracized as a child because it was rumored that His birth was illegitimate. Therefore, Christ first tasted the very thing that He came to champion in people's lives.

22. Harper Lee, *To Kill a Mockingbird* (New York: Popular Library, 1962), 49.

23. Heb. 7:26 NIV; Matt 11:19.

24. Quoted in Ian Thomas, *The Indwelling Life of Christ: All of Him in All of Me* (Sisters, OR: Multnomah, 2006), iii.

25. John 5:39 NLT.

26. John Wesley, in a letter to Joseph Benson, 7 November 1768, in *The Letters of the Rev. John Wesley*, ed. John Telford (London: Epworth Press, 1960), 5:110.

27. The Old Testament was written to the people of Israel. The New Testament was written to various churches and believing communities. Only six books in the New Testament were written to individuals: Philemon, 1 and 2 Timothy, Titus, 3 John, and Jude.

28. This line of thinking corrals atheists and Christians together into a unison choir to sing from the same epistemological song sheet. For most of Christian history, it was thought that every passage of Scripture had at least four meanings.

29. The specifics on *how* to live by the Lord's indwelling life are well beyond the scope of this book. However, the Lord's life can be starved and neglected within the believer. He can be ignored to our own spiritual loss.

Chapter 9: A House of Figs

1. Eph. 3:10.
2. 1 Cor. 1:24.
3. See John 20:17.
4. Eph. 3:18–19. See also Ephesians 1:22–23.
5. 1 Cor. 12:12.
6. Dietrich Bonhoeffer, *Act and Being: Transcendental Philosophy and Ontology in Systematic Theology*, ed. Hans-Richard Reuter, in volume 2 of *The Works of Dietrich Bonhoeffer* (Minneapolis: Fortress Press, 1996), 111, 112, 115.
7. Acts 9:4, emphasis added.
8. See 1 Corinthians 3:11–13.
9. A. B. Simpson, as quoted in Albert Edward Thompson, *The Life of A. B. Simpson* (New York: Christian Alliance Publishing Co., 1920), 196.
10. Rom. 16:25; Eph. 3:9; 6:19; Col. 1:25–29; 4:3.
11. Frank Viola's ReChurch series discusses this concept in great detail. For details, visit www.ReimaginingChurch.org.
12. John 1:11.
13. Luke 13:34.
14. Luke 9:51–53.
15. Mark 6:4.
16. John 7:5. Interestingly, Jesus asked no one from His first thirty years to be His disciple.
17. Luke 9:58.
18. T. Austin-Sparks points this out in his book *The Centrality and Supremacy of the Lord Jesus Christ* (Bethesda, MA: Testimony Book Ministry, 1989), 23–24.
19. He also found there the beauty and the music of the seashore.
20. Isa. 66:1.
21. The last verse of G. K. Chesterton, "The House of Christmas," in his *Collected Poetry*, Part 1, ed. Aidan Mackey, 10, from *The Collected Works of G. K. Chesterton*, vol. 10 (San Francisco: Ignatius Press, 1994), 140.
22. Matt. 10:40; Mark 9:37; Luke 10:16; John 13:20.
23. 1 Cor. 1:12–13.
24. Radcliffe, *Why Go to Church?* 79.
25. John 15:15.
26. Mark 12:29–30.
27. 2 Cor. 4:10–12.
28. 2 Cor. 12:7–9.
29. God's house is made up of cleansed lepers. That's what we all are. We were inflicted with the disease of spiritual leprosy, an apt metaphor for sin. But Jesus Christ touched and healed us.

30. We are referring to "the Lord's Table," His body in the form of the Eucharist (Communion), as well as His physical body laid out in the tomb.

31. Anointing a dead body with perfume was done to prepare it for burial. The perfume would cover up the smell of the decaying corpse. Kings were anointed for burial by having perfume poured upon them from the head down. This is what Mary did for Jesus. It was as if, without even realizing it, she understood that the Lord wouldn't be with them much longer.

32. Phil. 3:8 NIV.

33. 2 Cor. 2:14 NIV.

34. John 12:3.

35. See John 12:4–6.

36. Mark 11:1–10.

37. Mark 11:11.

38. Mark 11:12–13.

39. Mark 11:19; Matt. 21:17.

40. The word may also have the meaning of "house of affliction" or "house of the poor."

41. John 1:11.

42. Eph. 1:20–23.

43. Eph. 2:5–6.

44. John 7:39; Acts 2:33.

45. John 14:16–20; 1 Cor. 15:45.

46. Eph. 1:22.

Chapter 10: Who Is This Lord of Yours?

1. For those who reject the Trinity (a post-apostolic term that was used to describe the true God), we suggest the following books, all of which make a strong biblical and historical case for the reality of the Godhead in Scripture: James R. White, *The Forgotten Trinity* (Minneapolis, MN: Bethany House, 1998); Stanley Grenz, *Theology for the Community of God* (Nashville: Broadman and Holman, 1994); Kevin Giles, *The Trinity and Subordinationism* (Downers Grove, IL: InterVarsity Press, 2002); Giles, *Jesus and the Father* (Grand Rapids: Zondervan, 2006); Gilbert Bilezikian, *Community 101* (Grand Rapids: Zondervan, 1997); Ted Peters, *God as Trinity* (Louisville, KY: Westminster/John Knox Press, 1993).

2. See Leonard Sweet, *So Beautiful: Divine Design for Life and the Church* (Colorado Springs: David C. Cook, 2009); Sweet, *The Three Hardest Words in the World to Get Right* (Colorado Springs: Waterbrook, 2006); and Frank Viola, *Reimagining Church: Pursuing the Dream of Organic Christianity* (Colorado Springs: David C. Cook, 2008).

3. Immanuel Kant, *The Conflict of the Faculties: Der Streit der Fakultäten*, trans. Mary J. Gregor (New York: Abaris Books, 1979), 65.

4. The historic church called this divine dance and coinherence of Father, Son, and Spirit the *perichoresis*. For a great discussion on the relationship of the triune God to the church and the Christian life, see Milt Rodriguez, *The Community Life of God: Seeing the Godhead as the Model for All Relationships* (Gainesville, FL: The Rebuilders, 2009).

5. See Augustine, *The Trinity* (viii, 8, 12), *Fathers of the Church: A New Translation* 45 (Washington D.C., Catholic University of America Press, 1963), 263–64.

6. John 14:6; Eph. 3:18–19.

7. John 1:1–3, 14, 18; 5:23; 14:9.

8. Col. 2:9.

9. Dietrich Bonhoeffer, *Ethics*, ed. Eberhard Bethge, trans. Neville Horton Smith (New York: Simon and Schuster, 1995), 192. Originally published in German [*Ethik*] in 1949, and in English in 1955. The excerpt is also found in *Dietrich Bonhoeffer: Witness to Jesus Christ*, ed. John W. DeGruchy (Minneapolis: Fortress Press, 1991), 238.

10. From Lemmel, "Turn Your Eyes Upon Jesus."

11. Luke 7:47, 50.

12. John 8:11.

13. 2 Cor. 4:7.

14. Lemmel, "Turn Your Eyes Upon Jesus."

15. Acts 10:38.

16. Quoted in Hugh Gilbert, *Unfolding the Mystery: Monastic Conferences on the Liturgical Year* (Leominster, Eng.: Gracewing, 2007), 119.

17. John 1:29.

18 Rev. 5:5.

19. Phil. 2:10–11.

20. See Matthew 24:30; Psalm 2:8; Daniel 7:14; John 5:22; Matthew 25:32; and 2 Corinthians 5:10.

21. 1 Tim. 6:14; 2 Tim. 4:8; Titus 2:13; 1 Peter 5:4.

22. John 17:22; Col. 3:4; 2 Thess. 1:10; 1 John 3:2; Rom. 8:17.

23. Rev. 1:7.

24. Rev. 11:15.

25. Phil. 2:8–11.

26. Credit for the language of a "new frontier" goes to John F. Kennedy.

27. To explore the fruit of Paul's gospel and revelation of Christ, see Frank Viola, *Finding Organic Church: A Comprehensive Guide to Starting and Sustaining Authentic Christian Communities* (Colorado Springs: David C. Cook, 2009).

28. Rev. 3:14.

29. Entry for May 19, in George McDonald, *A Book of Strife in the Form of the Diary of an Old Soul* (London: Printed for the Author, 1880), 103. With thanks to Alan Hirsch for reminding us of this poem.

30. John 9:25, emphasis added.

31. The third verse of Charles Wesley, "Hark, the Herald Angels Sing," as found in *The Methodist Hymnal: The Official Hymnal of the Methodist Episcopal Church and the Methodist Episcopal Church, South* (New York: Methodist Book Concern, 1905), 111.

32. With thanks to Chris Hyslop and Thomas Merton for giving us the idea for this metaphor. Thomas Merton once prayed, "My Lord God, I have no idea where I am going. I do not see the road ahead of me. I cannot know for certain where it will end. I will not fear, for You are ever with me, and You will never leave me to face my perils alone." (Thomas Merton, *Thoughts in Solitude* [New York: Farrar, Straus and Giroux, 1999], 79.)

CONNECTING

F or more resources, book specials, events, and more about the authors, go to *www.theJesusManifesto.com*. Be sure to fill out the "Receive Updates" form to receive periodic updates from the authors.

ABOUT THE AUTHORS

Leonard Sweet currently occupies the E. Stanley Jones Chair of Evangelism, serving from 1995 to 2001 as vice president of academic affairs and dean of the Theological School at Drew University, Madison, New Jersey. A visiting distinguished professor at George Fox University in Portland, Oregon, and president emeritus of United Theological Seminary, he is a weekly contributor to the online preaching resource www.sermons.com.

Author of more than two hundred articles, twelve hundred published sermons, and almost forty books, Sweet is the author of two textbooks: one on preaching, *Giving Blood*, and one on evangelism, *Nudge: Awakening Each Other to the God Who Is Already There*. He is also the author of *So Beautiful: Divine Design for Life and the Church*, and his weekly podcast is "Napkin Scribbles." Leonard is designated one of "The Twitter Elite" routinely ranking in the top thousand of the millions of Twitter and Facebook users worldwide.

F rank Viola is a frequent conference speaker and the author of numerous books on the deeper Christian life and church renewal. His books include *From Eternity to Here*, *Finding Organic Church*, *Reimagining Church*, and *The Untold Story of the New Testament Church*. Frank's Web site, www.frankviola.com, contains many free resources that will help you implement the insights in this book, including audio messages, an interactive blog, a monthly eNewsletter, articles, and more. Frank and his family live in Gainesville, Florida.

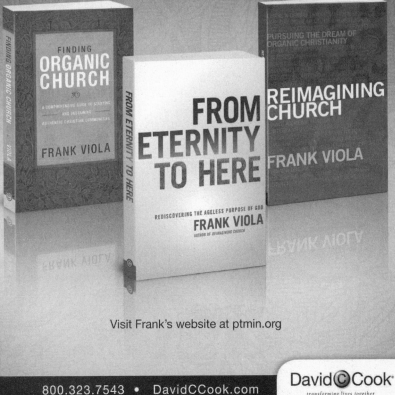